MI'SEL

AN ABORIGINAL CHIEF'S JOURNEY

JOE

MI'SEL

AN ABORIGINAL CHIEF'S JOURNEY

JOE

COMPILED AND EDITED BY

RAOUL R. ANDERSEN AND JOHN K. CRELLIN

FLANKER PRESS LTD.

ST. JOHN'S

2009

Library and Archives Canada Cataloguing in Publication

Joe, Mi'sel, 1947-
Mi'sel Joe : an aboriginal chief's journey / edited by Raoul R. Andersen
and John K. Crellin.

Includes bibliographical references and index.
ISBN 978-1-897317-42-6

1. Mi'sel, Joe, 1947-. 2. Micmac Indians--Newfoundland and Labrador--
Conne River--Kings and rulers--Biography. 3. Micmac Indians--Newfoundland
and Labrador--Conne River--Biography. 4. Micmac Indians--Biography.
I. Andersen, Raoul, 1936- II. Crellin, J. K. III. Title.

PS8635.I355B33 2008   ,   C813'.6   C2008-904360-X

PRINTED IN CANADA

Cover Design: Adam Freake

FLANKER PRESS
PO BOX 2522, STATION C
ST. JOHN'S, NL, CANADA
TOLL FREE: 1-866-739-4420
WWW.FLANKERPRESS.COM

15 14 13 12 11 10 09   1 2 3 4 5 6 7 8 9 10

We acknowledge the financial support of the Government of Canada through the Book Publishing
Industry Development Program (BPIDP) for our publishing activities; the Canada Council for the
Arts which last year invested $20.1 million in writing and publishing throughout Canada; the
Government of Newfoundland and Labrador, Department of Tourism, Culture and Recreation.

For all
Our People

"When people appreciate their own history, that's healthy."

Contents

Preface xi

1: Worlds Apart 1

At the time I didn't think we were being oppressed 1
I learned to fear outside authorities 7
I can't remember ever being hungry 9
I wasn't sickly or anything 14
Borrowing things between families was common 15
In the early days, we lived along the lines of the clan system 16
The choice was to go to work 18
In 1964, I figured this is enough Newfoundland stuff 20
The hardest part of all was the loss of dignity 25
Working on the tracks 27
Trying to find me 29
They used to call me the Newfoundland Tonto 32
I was one of those picked to go to Churchill Falls 37
I wanted to be able to smell the woods again 41
I had found out how to go all around that circle 43

2: Struggle for Dignity 47

The whole picture of chief came forward 47
We had to learn how to heal ourselves 56
I had a vision experience 57
White caribou 60
A welfare issue 62
People began to lose sight of pulling together 63
The walk 68

3: Recovering Traditional Values and Ways 75

The conflict took a toll for a long time 75

The sweat lodge 76
Ceremonies 79
Sentencing circles 81
The Mi'kmaq always had a seasonal routine 82
Women were powerful in the community 85
Lots of our history is connected to Miquelon 90
There are still wakes at home 94
In many ways we were no different 96
Stories of Mount Sylvester 97
If you want a cure, Bay Nord was the place to go 99
For everyday things people used the plants we have 102
We need to let people know what we are doing 105
Our Stonehenge is our wigwam and our canoe 110
Voyages 115
The Pow-wow connects us to the past 120
Children must be part of our tradition 123
Many of our traditions are coming alive again 126

4: Community Services 129

Spiritual and community journeys 129
The Clinic is the hub of our community services 130
Child and youth services 133
Our elders are as important to us as our children 134
When an elder walks through the door 138
We built what we called a "Spiritual Building" 139
We no longer have our own police 140
Employment is an important aspects of a person's dignity 141
Developing life skills is important for our community 142
Job creation means we have to be entrepreneurs 144
The Band Council's projects must have support 146

5: Journeys and the Future 149

My journey has really been many journeys 149

Acknowledgements 155
Bibliography 157
About Mi'sel Joe 164
About the Editors 165
Index 167

Illustrations

Map of Conne River region xviii
Map of Atlantic Canada xix
Mi'sel Joe dressed for confirmation 6
Tractor driving on Lever Brothers Mushroom Farm 31
Mi'sel Joe at the Calgary Stampede 33
On King's Ranch, High River, Alberta 33
Michael Joe Sr. and Martin Jeddore 45
Newspaper clippings surrounding the hunger strike 55
Meeting the Grand Chief, Donald Marshall, Sr. 71
Photograph of two Mi'kmaq guides (c. 1907) 84
ATVs, today's vehicles for hunting 84
Classes on trapping and preparing skins 85
Basket making class 90
Old church at Conne River, early 1900s 93
Matteau and Uncle Mick (c. 1950s) 93
Rebuilt church in Conne River, photographed in 1998 94
Birchbark wigwam on the Medicine Trail 103
Drummers, choir, and dancers of Conne River (c. 1990s) 106
Drummers chanting (c. 2000) 106
Hawaiian double-hulled canoe, 1995 108
Birch bark ready for construction 111
Collecting spruce roots 111
Canoe under construction 112
Symbolic eagle 112
The *Spirit Wind* 113
Birchbark canoe and water plane 113
Trial run in canoe with MP Roger Simmons 116
Visiting Mi'kmaq craftsman fashioning a canoe paddle 119
Poster advertising Conne River Pow-wow of 1996 120
Mi'sel Joe at Pow-wow 2000 121
"Wigwam hotel" during the 1998 Pow-wow 122
Brenda Jeddore rehearsing choir at St. Anne's School, 1990s 124
A scene from St. Anne's School Pow-wow 124

Mi'sel Joe's liner notes for choir's CD 125
Mi'sel Joe talking with students 127
Band Council Building 132
Calendar recognizing knowledge and experience of elders 135
Information leaflets highlighting Band Clinic's services 137
The "Spiritual Building," photographed 1998 140
Entertaining the captain of a cruise ship (2007) 145
Mi'sel Joe working on a canoe paddle (1996) 147
Mi'sel Joe greets Pope John Paul II in St. John's, 1984 150
SCB Fisheries building (c. 2000) 153
Reconnecting with Miquelon (2004) 154

Preface

SAQAMAW OR CHIEF Mi'sel Joe (b. 1947), traditional and elected chief of Newfoundland and Labrador's Conne River Mi'kmaq, tells of his encounters with Canadian society, rediscovery of his people's culture, and the development of his community – the Conne River Reserve or, more properly, the Miawpukek First Nation. His story will touch the interests of a wide range of readers within the province of Newfoundland and Labrador, and all those with a general interest in aboriginal affairs, community health, and revitalization.

The chief's story is about a changing life and community. He admits that he is only one witness to the events and circumstances described. After all, no single individual owns the whole story. It is an oral history, a personal account, and, like written history, it is incomplete. What he tells us does not explore the intricacies of such matters as negotiations and differing visions within and between the Conne River band and provincial and federal levels of government, but it adds important perspective. Rather, its focus reflects our shared desire to capture the growing awareness of Mi'kmaq traditions, values and spirituality within the Conne River community.

Conne River people and Mi'kmaq elsewhere in

Newfoundland and Labrador and on the mainland have undergone centuries of assaults by European colonization, government and Church policies, and other social forces that have undermined and alienated them from their traditional beliefs, values and practices. Readers with a particular interest in the nature of change will find Chief Joe's knowledge of and search for his people's traditional ways especially instructive when compared with historical accounts of Mi'kmaq culture.

Our early interest in the Conne River community coincided with a time of great stress for countless communities in Newfoundland arising from the 1992 federal moratorium on the Northern cod commercial fishery due to overfished stocks. It was probably no mere coincidence that the reassertion of traditional Mi'kmaq values and the need for respect coincided with the Conne River community's development of grassroots self-government and programs for economic sustainability. The themes of recovery, sustainability, and the building of "healthy" communities were in the air. The Conne River community was doing just that. Of course, we are not saying that tensions did not arise, some of which were in terms of "traditionalists" versus "non-traditionalists" (or "moderns"), but they became less and less disruptive. Such tensions are widely met and perhaps inevitable in all community development.

We felt it was important to capture Mi'sel Joe's own words for specific reasons aside from a life story. One is that his recollections of Newfoundland life add perspective to familiar Newfoundland history such as accessing health care, the demise of midwifery, and the public health voyages of the *Christmas Seal*, also known as the "TB ship." Another reason is because of the variety of ways in which Chief Joe is viewed – as a "healer," as a leader, as an astute politician. People, many from outside his community, who see him as a healer are not so much interested in traditional medicines (this knowledge has been largely lost to the community), but as a spiritual healer in ways that cross religious boundaries. Much of that lies in his "teaching" about values and spirituality – often seen in his stories and reflections – that many find to be "holistic," something they themselves are searching for.

Mi'sel Joe is a recognized leader by virtue of being both traditional chief (conferred by the Mi'kmaq Grand Chief) and, over the years, administrative chief (elected biennially). As such, questions arise about the separate roles of each. How often and where do they meld? How is this different from the traditional leadership of the past? How does having both roles affect political decision making? While this oral memoir is that of a First Nations leader in an aboriginal community in the most eastern province of Canada, much of it will resonate with all aboriginal people, whether living on or off reserves. His accounts of early life in Conne River and migratory work on the mainland offer testimony to entrenched contradictions in Euro-North American society; industry recruits aboriginal labour (often at low wages), while prejudice and stereotyping, and perhaps fear, have created a surfeit of hardships for countless aboriginal people and stolen their dignity.

At the same time, the memoir as a whole will resonate with many non-aboriginal communities today, large and small, as they struggle to provide their citizens with fundamental opportunities, services, and security. This is often difficult, especially for small rural communities where declining industry and employment trigger a chain of challenging consequences that include outmigration, aging populations, and reduced health, education, and social services. It is noteworthy that today many people – including government officials – recognize Conne River as a "success" story, a "model," in the creation of a healthy community. This is in the face of the special difficulties facing First Nations communities. Across Canada, regardless of their treaty and other rights, aboriginal communities have been disrupted, if not eliminated, with loss of traditional lands and languages. Land claims linger on, unresolved, for decades. Aboriginal children often receive inadequate formal education, and rates of unemployment, family instability, domestic violence, substance abuse, and suicide exceed national averages.

* * *

Mi'sel Joe graciously agreed to let us tape-record his memories and reflections after a number of collaborative activities between the Conne River Community and Memorial University during the 1990s. The activities included traditional medicine conferences, educational trips to England and Hawaii, and the development of opportunities for medical students to visit the Conne River community to better understand health issues. His story, recorded over a number of years, then transcribed and silently edited, falls into five chapters; together they offer a sense of the richness of Mi'kmaq culture before it was suppressed by the priests, especially Father Stanley St. Croix, and finally conscious attention to the revitalization of past traditions that fit into the modern world.

In the first chapter, Mi'sel Joe tells of his early life in the isolated Conne River community in Bay d'Espoir on Newfoundland's south coast, and, secondly, as a young man going west to mainland Canada. There, in a migratory work pattern with occasional respites back in Conne River, he experienced a wide range of jobs – ranching, the railroad, mining, operating heavy equipment, logging, and commercial fishing. It was a time of self-discovery and learning amid loneliness, disillusion, stereotyping, and repeated episodes of illness and recovery. In the second chapter, he tells of a major clash with the provincial government that precipitated some band members to go on hunger strike, and a period of discord within the community. The remaining chapters focus on traditional ways, and community development that has been underpinned not only by increasingly effective self-government and commercial initiatives, but also by a continuing effort to appreciate traditional values.

Each page of Chief Joe's account raises questions for further enquiry, especially about the search for identity in a changing world. His story contributes to literature both by Mi'kmaq and non-Mi'kmaq people (some is noted in the annotated bibliography). We hope the account will encourage other Mi'kmaq people, both on and off reserves, to add their voices and reflections on their own community journeys.

* * *

A few notes are added here as historical perspective on the Newfoundland Mi'kmaq, who are the most easterly extension of contemporary Algonquian–speaking peoples in North America. Their primary historical identity in Newfoundland, as a hunting and trapping people, contrasts with that of Newfoundland's white European people in onshore and offshore commercial fisheries. Just how long they have been a presence in Newfoundland remains an issue of historical debate, as made clear in Mi'sel Joe's comments. In this century, the decline of the fur trade, industrialization, and non-native or settler competition reduced Mi'kmaq dependency upon the land, and they entered occupations like forestry, construction, mining, and even commercial fishing.

By the early 1900s, Conne River was the major settlement and perhaps refuge of the island's traditional Mi'kmaq people. Conne River Mi'kmaq remember well a history of Church and Newfoundland government actions that stigmatized and nearly obliterated their aboriginal cultural identity, abolished their designated community under the Newfoundland government in the 1930s, and attempted to assimilate them – albeit as a marginalized people – into Newfoundland and Canadian non-aboriginal society. Confederation with Canada in 1949 should have brought federal recognition and support of the Mi'kmaq people. However, official recognition of Newfoundland Mi'kmaq as aboriginals did not occur until the early 1970s. Only in the 1980s did the Conne River Mi'kmaq gain a direct federal relationship, registered aboriginal status, and reserve community status under Canada's Indian Act.

Today the Conne River Band of over 700 occupies a small reserve about 30 miles inland from Newfoundland's south coast in Bay d'Espoir. It is a historic summer camping place and an access point to the island interior's rich hunting and trapping grounds, and nearby waters abound in marine game and waterfowl.

Band members maintain relations with other Mi'kmaq elsewhere in Newfoundland and mainland Mi'kmaq bands in Nova Scotia, New Brunswick, and eastern Quebec. This reflects historical connections and understandings that Newfoundland Mi'kmaq originated on the mainland. The island-mainland relationship is part of the process of ongoing search for, discovery, reinvention, and consolidation of Mi'kmaq cultural identity and religious and spiritual life, and a key aspect of their political strength as a First Nation in Canadian society. Mi'sel Joe's personal story exemplifies this ongoing search, especially his roles as chief. But his is only one case among a people whose traditions permit and encourage spiritual self-discovery and harmony.

RRA and JKC

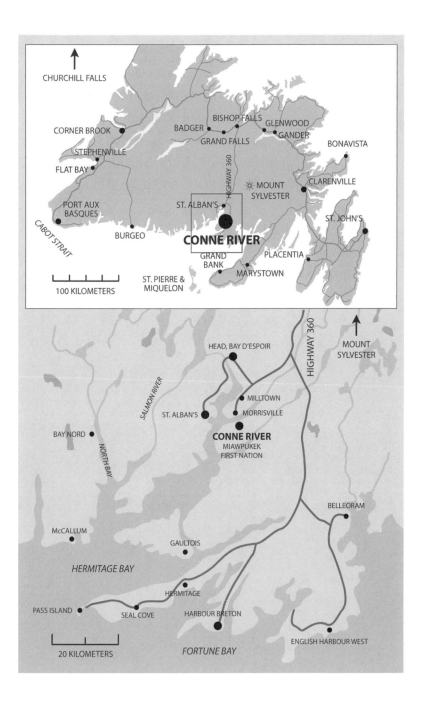

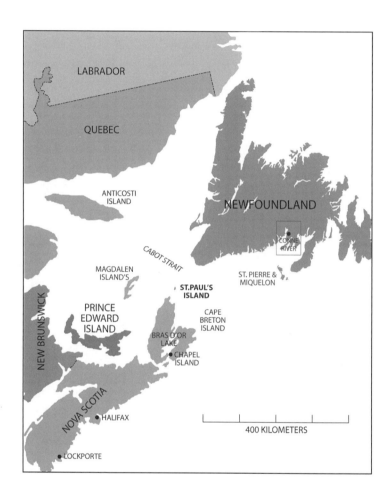

Left: A map showing Conne River and surrounding area.

Top: A map showing areas in Atlantic Canada pertinent to the
    Conne River Mi'kmaq, and recent canoe trips. See pp. xix, 91,
    108, 109, 115–119, 123, 149, 154, 157, 158

Conne River.

1

Worlds Apart

At the time I didn't think we were being oppressed.
More now, not then. It affected your ability to deal
with people. You could probably take care of your-
self in the earlier years. I remember the first time
when we were going outside of Conne River.
Everything was foreign. I couldn't talk to people, I
didn't know what to do. I didn't know how to talk
to people. It was instilled in you so bad, I had this
fear of anyone who was a doctor, a priest, RCMP,
someone from the government, or even if you
worked for someone, like a foreman. I was 15
years old and I was so afraid of foreigners that if
one said I had to swim across the Gander River I
probably would have. That was the kind of thing
you had to live with.

I STARTED SCHOOL in Conne River when I was seven years old
– that was in 1954. It was a one-room building. I thought it was
big at the time but it wasn't. It might have been thirty or forty
feet long. Before we got grade nine, they came in and put a par-
tition across the room that you could haul together. So the

higher grades were on one side and the lower grades on the other.

There was only one teacher. She taught everybody. Boys and girls were all in the same class. Each student had to bring splits of wood from home into the school every day for making the fire. You had no choice. Two boys in class had to make the fire for one week. You made it around seven o'clock in the morning and got the place warmed up for nine o'clock.

What I remember most fondly about the school was storytime. The stories were for the higher grades, and we were told to sit there and do whatever we had to do in grade one, two, or three. While the teacher read the story, I'd sit there and listen and it was the most pleasant part of the day. Apart from that you were either freezing or too hot, or you were being knocked up the side of the head with a book or a duster or stick or something. The only interest I had in school was history and geography and things like that, which I excelled in really well. In the other ones I was a complete washout.

The one thing I hated most was catechism. You had to be able to memorize pages of that every night. And come back next morning and repeat your question and answer. We used to get the questions all mixed up. When you were called on to recite, you had to keep your head down, look at the floor, and the teacher would pat you on the back. "Good. Sit down." And on to the next one. Some students really learned the catechism, but they used to mumble the answer; we were told we couldn't speak very good English anyway. The teacher referred to our broken English as mumbling. So we developed a way of saying our catechism without saying anything at all. Whole pages of it.

We did pretty good. We managed to use that to our advantage. The teachers either didn't care or whatever, and we got by. We'd have a chuckle afterwards over what we were mumbling about. It was nonsense. Nothing to do with the question. It was such a small, little world we had there that it wasn't very devastating when the teacher said, "You're not very smart," or "You're dirty," or "You can't speak very good." It sort of fit everybody.

Before they added the extra grades at Conne River, if you wanted to go beyond grade seven you had to go to the school across the bay in St. Alban's. I wouldn't go, but my younger brother tried to. He found it was such a hard thing because of the racism and he just left. Other students went and got through it. Maybe they had family there that they could go to. But we had very few family in St. Alban's, and my brother had to come home when he got kicked out of the boarding house on weekends, as that wasn't paid for. You either stayed outside or found someplace to stay for the weekend. So the first time that happened, he came home and wouldn't go back.

My mother talked about how things couldn't be that bad. And how she grew up in the poor times in Conne River. In many ways, she had come through a life of agony because she looked after her mother, who died, looked after both of her sisters, who died of tuberculosis, and she had a family of nine children. She always said, "You got to go to school." "You got to get out of here." "You got to do better than that."

She always tried to encourage us to do better. She would perk us up when we were down. She was a strong woman. My dad talked about getting an education if he was just starting out. He'd go to school, get an education. He'd say, "You've got to get out of the woods." My mom and dad had about a grade two education, but they were able to read and write.

The teachers came from all over Newfoundland, but nine out of ten came from across the bay. Places like St. Alban's, Milltown, and other nearby communities. In earlier years some of the women stayed and married aboriginal men. Some were nasty when they first came to Conne River, but over time they mellowed and got better. Some didn't stay long, only the winter.

And even up to when the community took over our own school, a lot of the men that came there were brutal. Some came just to get the isolation pay and were what nobody else wanted anyway. There was no roads, the only way in to Conne River was by boat. Until the 1960s, there was no electricity, no telephones. We didn't even have radio when I was growing up, and television didn't arrive until the mid-sixties.

I remember one teacher I had. He must have been in his early twenties. He was a boozer. You could smell it off him. He really liked to throw people around. It didn't take much at all. Maybe because a guy didn't do his homework, or he couldn't answer a question, or couldn't spell, or couldn't read. It didn't take anything at all. One day, a Monday, he put one guy in the stove. It was one of those big, high black ones. And the teacher came down and opened the cover. He picked him up by his arms and put his head down inside. He didn't burn him, but it singed his hair.

And it was nothing for him to bounce you off the wall a half-dozen times. They would have you crawl on the floor on your hands and knees until you damned near passed out. And another thing we was made to do was to stand there with two big books, one in each hand, and every time you dropped one, you'd get it across the back with a big stick. He hit one fellow around my age so hard that he hurt his chest; he claims today that sometimes he still feels it in his chest.

Some of the girls had just as hard a time. Some teachers would strap them. One had an old hardwood desktop made of narrow strips of hardwood. He'd take a three-foot-long strip off the corner and beat your arms or hands with it. Or across the back, or up the side of your ankles. Or he'd throw books or erasers at you. And he'd walk behind you and hit you in the back. Push you around. That wasn't just happening to me; it was happening to other people as well.

Father St. Croix was gone before I was born, but the effects of his influence were still around in the attitudes and policies of the Church.* The priest was the ultimate power in the community and banned the use of our language and ceremonies; we couldn't even have our Indian names, only Christian names. If the teachers reported that they couldn't take care of you, then the priest came in and he made sure you did what they wanted. It was nothing for him to get violent, even to knock people off a wall.

We had some decent women teachers. But sometimes they would give pretty rough treatment; they knew they had the backing of the priest and that Mi'kmaq parents wouldn't say anything against them. If your child came home from school

* Father St. Croix served the Bay d'Espoir area parish from 1916–1946. He is remembered here for being highly intolerant of the Mi'kmaq language and culture, especially for its spiritual beliefs and rituals. He strictly enforced the use of English in school, strapped children if they spoke Mi'kmaq, and he banned its use in church. Rather than hold services in Conne River's community church, which was maintained by the chief and elders, he held them in a settler's house. As a result of the tensions he created, he is blamed for having driven the community's traditional chief, Noel Jeddore, and his family into permanent exile in Nova Scotia in 1925. (Doug Jackson 1993: 161; see also Dorothy Anger 1983: 75–78).

and couldn't walk, or couldn't write and couldn't cut wood because their hands were swollen, nothing was said about it. That's the way it was. You couldn't fight the priest. You couldn't fight the government.

At the time it was no big deal. It happened. It's only now that we look back and say that wasn't right. It didn't happen to everybody. There was some that probably put their head down and never looked up from the time they went to school till they left. They did all the things they were supposed to do. They learned their catechism and could repeat it word for word. And there were others who weren't in that category. I was one of them.

Mi'sel Joe (right), aged seven,
dressed for confirmation.

* * *

I learned to fear outside authorities maybe from going to church. I had no recollection then of Cornwallis's* orders in 1749 or whatever. My grandfather certainly knew that, and other people in the community knew that. And probably that fear comes from stories being told in the community as well. About Indians being hunted and not allowed to speak the language, and not allowed to sing our songs. We were born free, but no longer free.

The older people talked about it among themselves and you'd hear stories like that. Government was to be feared and the authorities would intrude. Like, when every time we'd see the RCMP show up it was to take someone away from the community for whatever reason. There's a story about my uncle. The RCMP came in because somebody reported that there was homebrew being made in the community, like all over Newfoundland. They came to Conne River to look for the homebrew and, when they went into my grandfather's house, they found a pan full of moose liver being cooked. They asked my grandfather whose it was. They found out it was my uncle who shot the moose and went after him; they told him, "We need the meat." Uncle took them in the woods and got the moose. He lugged it out for them and they took it away as evidence for illegal hunting. And this comes from people that was starving in most cases. And living in rags. I asked my uncle

* Edward Cornwallis (1713–1776) became governor of Nova Scotia in 1749. As part of his task to consolidate British claims, he went to war with the Mi'kmaqs. (See *Dictionary National Biography*, Oxford University Press.) "A premium of ten Guineas for every Indian killed or taken prisoner." (See, R. H. Whitehead 1991: 115–122).

about that a few years ago. "Why did you go and show them the moose meat?"

"Well, they wanted it." "You want it, you can have it. We can get some more."

They had to go to court, and some time later they showed up by boat, a cutter. They got Uncle off the floor. He had no bed. They were on the way to the door when they said, "You got to go back and get dressed."

"What for?"

"You can't go dressed like that."

"It's all I got."

The clothes in his bag were all he had. "The only thing I know is I'd have to go naked. I can't change my clothes because they're all I got."

They took him on the boat. On board was a magistrate. Well, they had other stops to make and took him on to St. John's. He served his time on the boat from Bay d'Espoir to St. John's and back. He had lots to eat every day, and the run of the ship. When he came back, he had new clothes and he wanted to go back. Such good treatment. Everybody wanted to go!

Those are interesting things about the RCMP coming to Conne River. Back then, it was "Here's what you're going to get. Like it or not." Recently I was able to tell their old top brass how matters had changed from being afraid of the RCMP, to running our local police – I talk about that later – and now with the RCMP stationed in Conne River with good communication with the public to prevent crime.

* * *

I can't remember ever being hungry. Not for very long, anyway. When salmon was around, we'd get them from the river. We often never brought any salmon home. Everybody who wanted salmon went there, caught some and cooked them and ate it right there. And when we wanted more salmon we'd go back again. So there was never hoarding. And it was always done by net. You'd put a little string of net across the river, throw rocks off in the pool, and get whatever was there. Sometimes we'd get none, one or two, or even three or four if you were lucky.

I have four brothers and four sisters. I'm the oldest brother, and two sisters are older than me. We lived in a good house when we were growing up. It was maybe 26 by 24 foot square, with a pitched roof. A saltbox house near the water. I was born at home, as most of us were. We thought it was very big. Downstairs, there was a big kitchen, a small sitting room, and a pantry. One thing I remember is that the upstairs was never finished. It had bedrooms, but also a sort of central place. During the winter months, we would have caribou or moose, even sometimes in the fall, hanging from the upstairs. Later on we had a shed outside and the meat would be hanging there. In our room where we slept, there was only lumber on one side and snow would drift in. There was extreme cold, especially when we'd get up in the morning with snow on the floor and on the bed. If you weren't sharing a bed with your brothers, you slept on the floor. A lot of times I slept on the floor behind the stove on a caribou skin. Everybody used it. In the spring, Mom made slippers or moccasins out of it.

I can't remember ever being hungry, but I certainly remember being cold. We had a root cellar lined with logs where we kept our potatoes and other vegetables. It had a hatch and sometimes my dad would put a cat in there for a few days to keep the rats and mice out. And I can't remember having too many "flus" or sickness like that. We seemed to have got along quite well. We had gardens, we had potatoes. And, in earlier years, we had chickens and eggs. My dad was a good hunter, so we always had something to eat, like moose meat. There was always something. In the summer we fished for salmon and eels, cod and flatfish. We speared eels. The spear was made of birch wood and rind. My grandfather and others used to make them. We fished along the river shore in dories at low tide. We went for eels at night, bring them home, clean them, hang them on the wall to dry, and they became supper the next day.

I remember we never tasted pork chops or chicken or anything like that until in the '60s, when all of a sudden we had electricity. The store could hold the meat for a long period of time because they had the freezers, but I remember my dad bringing home a slab of bacon and it made everybody sick. Just couldn't stand the smell of bacon frying, but he had been working for a long time in camps and to him it was common. And I remember how, on his last day of work before coming home, he would fill his pack with buns – molasses buns or cinnamon buns. He knew that when he left his pack on the porch, we would go out and rob it!

I remember my dad walking to Glenwood in May 1960, with Martin Jeddore, Guy McDonald, William John, and Eddy John. I was thirteen and wanted to go too, but my father said,

"No, someone has to stay home and get firewood and look after your mother." I didn't argue with him, just hung my head and walked away. Why me? I wondered. I didn't understand or really appreciate then what a sacred duty he was asking of me. But I stayed home and tried to look after my mom and family the best I could. I was up early on the morning when they started walking. They all had big bundles on their backs, and when they reached the top of the hill, against the sun that was just coming up, they looked like some strange creatures with big humps on their backs.

When he came home that fall we sat for hours listening to his stories about their walk of seven days to Glenwood. After three days they ran out of food and shot a beaver. The beaver floated near the beaver lodge, but it was a cold morning, so no one in the group wanted to go out after it. My dad volunteered to climb out on a tree that was hanging over the water, and just as he got over the beaver, the tree crashed into the lake. He came up spitting water and mud but holding the beaver. My dad had left home that time with the only suit he had packed in his bundle, so that night he wore it while his wet clothes dried as they sat around a fire, and cooked and ate the beaver meat. But when one young fellow said he couldn't eat it because it was Friday – he was that afraid of what the priests taught him – one of the older men told him, "Well, you'd better eat it now, because it won't be here next day."

The Northwest River was still high from spring runoff when they came down off the high country, so they cut a big dry pine, made a raft, and tied it together with their bundle straps and roots they dug along the river. The raft took all their gear down to the mouth of the river. After they reached the lake, they traded their raft for a boat ride across the lake to Glenwood.

When we were growing up, we went out to snare rabbits on Saturday, after school. But hunting wasn't a sport. If you were lucky enough to shoot a rabbit or partridge, that was for dinner on Sunday. I remember my dad brought home a nice, used pair of ice skates, the first pair seen around the community. You'd skate with your boots on. "Hockey skates," we called them. One day my cousin was passing with his .22 rifle and I gave him my skates for the .22.

My dad asked me, "Where's the skates?"

I said, "I traded them."

"For what?"

"A .22."

"How come?"

"Well, you can't shoot partridge with a pair of skates."

Moose hunting was in the fall. And if you were lucky, you'd be asked along by an uncle or somebody. I spent a lot of time with my uncle Lawrence, my dad's younger brother. We'd go in the woods, hunting and trapping and exploring. You'd bring home your share of meat that way. We never looked at it as a sport or anything other than providing.

Andrew Joe was my grandfather on my father's side. He was a big man. Pretty close to six foot tall. I don't know what happened to me, but he was fairly big! He was a very quiet gentleman, born and grew up in a wigwam on the land. My other grandfather on my mom's side, Paul Nicholas Jeddore, married Anne Joe. They were married in Norris Arm. They moved to Badger, and from there they walked to Conne River carrying my mom on their back. My grandfather Joe took me back on the traplines a couple of times, and when he went to cut firewood. Grandmother used to go along too sometimes. She was a midwife who was gone a lot. When she was at home, they seemed to be extremely close and they talked and chuckled a lot out in the dory. We'd gather firewood along the coast, and my grandmother would go along and pick up driftwood in the dory. We'd have our tea along the way. My grandfather was very strong and very gentle. Always singing Mi'kmaq hymns and other songs. But he didn't talk Mi'kmaq to me for some reason. I listened to him talking Mi'kmaq to my Uncle and other older people in the community; we didn't hear the language in my house very much, only when older people came to visit.

My mother understood the language, but she didn't speak very much of it. She'd talk to my grandfather. If he asked her something in Mi'kmaq she would answer in English. And when one of the older ladies came by, sometimes a lot of the conversation was in Mi'kmaq, and we'd think they were talking about women things. When we got older we realized that not too long after our *n'me* came we would have another brother or sister.*

Grandmother Joe, as I said, was the midwife in Conne River for many years. We knew that when Ma Joe showed up and drove everyone outside, including my father, we would soon have a new sister or brother. What I remember most about those years was when she moved in with us for three weeks, and before the three weeks was up someone would come and get her to go to another house. We would miss the great soup and homemade bread she would make.

* *N'me*: In the Nova Scotia Mikmaq lexicon, the word means "Granny," and is a term of affection for an older woman. (Deblois and Metalic 1984: 237.) Here, she also has special powers to heal or harm.

* * *

I wasn't sickly or anything, but I just remember having to go to the nearest hospital in Harbour Breton, but Mother often reminded me about what happened. I was very young at the time.

Nowadays Harbour Breton is an hour drive away. Then it took two or three days because it was too rough to go overland, so they usually had to go around by boat. I couldn't have been any older than four years and my face was swollen so bad I couldn't see. My father, my uncle, and Sylvester Jeddore took me to the hospital by boat. We travelled all night; we first landed at Gaultois, then Hermitage, then on to Harbour Breton. After we landed there was still a long way to walk to the hospital and for the last three or four miles everyone took turns carrying me on their back to the hospital where I spent the next two weeks. I had this abscess on my neck that caused the swelling. They didn't know what it was; they had to find out.

They shipped me back by the same route. One of my aunts came to get me by coastal boat. And I remember the smell of the hospital, how it was all white, and sitting with someone looking out of the window.

I don't remember visiting nurses or doctors on any regular basis. What I remember mostly was the *Christmas Seal*, the boat that came and took X-rays checking for TB. That was a problem in our community. The *Christmas Seal* would show up in the arm of the bay, and it would anchor in the middle of the river, so to speak. They then played Irish music, jigs and reels, on the loud speakers. We would gather around the beach and dance as long as they played the music, or we just listened. It was something that was unreal for us. We never heard anything like that before. And the other big thrill of course was actually getting to go aboard this huge vessel. I always remember being impressed with how clean and white it was. And the smell – it smelled clean. Our little boats were so different. It was a big thing when the *Christmas Seal* came around.

* * *

Borrowing things between families was common.
Growing up in Conne River, like in other places,
there were jealousies among the families. There
were people that helped each other to make sure
everybody had something. They went out of their
way to make sure that, if you had no sugar or
flour or butter, like some older people, they'd give
it to you. But some families would never do that.
They'd say, "I'm sorry. I don't care if you do go
hungry. All I got is enough for me."

Growing up, if you were out of butter and you got sent to a family to borrow a stick of butter, you'd say, I'll be back with the butter next month, or next day, or next weekend. I'd gladly go to my grandmother's place – she was all kindness – or my uncle's, and it would be no problem at all. But for most men it was dignity and pride in taking care of family and friends and community because that's what it was all about. It wasn't just about hoarding what you had just for you. That didn't fit what an aboriginal family was all about. But, in the community there were some families, people used to talk about them, that were extremely poor; there was something about them that nobody helped them, or nobody could help them. They just stayed extremely poor.

In Conne River they were very religious people and went to church, but I won't say a lot. In those days when growing up, the priest only came down about once every two or three months, especially on St. Anne's Day, July 26. It was a week-long celebration in the community, everybody tried to go to church every day and take part in what's happening. The priest, of course, had a different authority, right direct from God or direct from Rome. He could do anything, whatever he wanted, with everybody. Soul and otherwise.

* * *

In the early days, we lived along the lines of the "clan system." Today, in politics that same family cluster is still together and, nine times out of ten, how one family votes is generally how the whole clan votes. In the clan system, the grandmother would be out talking, telling what everybody could do. And they probably still do that in the majority of cases. The grandmothers are very influential.

I was still fairly young – 11 years old – when my grandfather Joe died. My grandmother died in 1989; she was 98 years old. I don't remember my grandmother Jeddore, I only know of her through stories that were told to me by my mother. Grandfather Jeddore died in the early '70s, but, I never had quite the same kind of close relationship with him as with my grandfather Joe. I never really thought much about it or understood how the clan system works until I got older.* If a father built a house and had twenty children, they all built around that same cluster. Each family had eight or ten families whose boss was a woman. My grandmother and great-grandmother were women who were pretty forceful in speaking out.

The only time we went outside the Joe clan, it was a rivalry sort of thing with other clans. I know we didn't venture into the Jeddore section too much until we got older. If you happened to go into it when you were younger, you got driven away, back home. You got sent back to your own. And I knew if we caught someone our own age on our side of the river, we'd drive them away with rocks. They weren't allowed unless they were older. Then we had no control over them. As we were growing up, we heard that the Joe clan were rough-and-tumble boys.

The clan still works in many ways like they used to. It votes as a group, like a voting block, like the way that families, the clusters, get together. They talk, and Conne River is not a very secretive place. If somebody is going to vote for somebody, it's all out in the open before. No secret about it in most cases.

* * *

* Here "clan" is colloquial usage. It refers to members of households related through the male line (patrilineal). (Cf. Harald E. L. Prins 1996: 32–33).

The choice was to go to work. *I stayed at school till I ran away. I just got tired of being beaten, I guess, and the last time I went back to school, I was 14 years old. My mother said to me, "Everybody's going to be in trouble if you don't go to school." She was talking about the government or the priest showing up. I remember I was sitting in the kitchen and she said, "I'm going to get the teacher. If you don't go to school, I'm going to get in trouble." She went after the teacher and said, "You'd better come and get him." And it wasn't very long before in came the teacher, who marched me off to school. I went, but I walked out again. I said, "No way." I wouldn't go back anymore.*

When I left school my dad was home. He said, "If you don't go to school, you got one other choice." That choice was to go to work. Dad worked with a pulpwood contractor at Glenwood, and he decided they would take me there with him. I had my birthday just when I got there, so I started cutting pulp when I was 15. By that time, there was no longer any camps or horses. It was just a contractor and machinery, staying in a boarding house, and our meals were prepared for us there or in a shack somewhere. My first week in the woods, I sawed my knee with a power saw and ended up off work for three weeks. So Dad took care of me and paid all our bills while he worked.

When I got better I went back to work, and we spent the summer there. Cutting pulp is a hard business. We worked six days a week. On Sunday you slept, at least I did, recovered, and on Monday you started all over again. We didn't get paid very much. You had to be 17 to get an EI card. So my dad paid the room and board, and gave me a little bit of money. Not much. A little bit. Change.

My father worked in the woods all his life, and he was strong; he could cut five or six cords a day with an old bucksaw. We used a power saw. My job was to cut the log knots off each junk with a pulpwood axe, and pile them up. That was my job. Sometimes he'd cut extra cords and I'd make a brow (pile) of them. He called them "ante" for the next day's work. It got to be a bit of a competition there. When he was cutting the last junk in the evening, I wanted to be right there and put it on the pile so he didn't have to wait for me. But I wasn't competing with him that first year.

In my second year, my dad said, "This summer I'm either going to make you or break you." He was saying that this is not the kind of life anyone would want. You do this if you got to do it, and that's it. He bought me a power saw and said, "You're on your own. It's a lot different now. I'm not paying your room and board. You got to pay your own way, your own gas, your own power saw." And then, after 12 days of cutting, when they came out with the scale on the wood, he had 58 cords of wood and I had 56. He left me alone after that!

That's the kind of work my dad did. He was a logger, a very hard worker, and he didn't tolerate anyone being lazy. He hunted and trapped during the winter months and went cutting pulp during the summer months. I didn't do much hunting and trapping with him. I spent more time with my grandfather and my uncles than my dad. When he was younger he couldn't tolerate too many kids around, especially when it come time to clean beavers. Beaver was precious in terms of feeding a family, and you couldn't have kids around that might fool it up and spoil the fur. He told me later, "That's what my father did to me, too. When I cleaned my first beaver, I did my own beaver. If I wanted to spoil it, that was my own business, but I wasn't allowed to spoil his." It makes more sense to me now than it did then. You learned on your own.

* * *

In 1964, I figured this is enough of this Newfoundland stuff. I'm heading west. Something was drawing me to the outside. Maybe I wanted to find out if everyone out there lived the way we did. One day, I planned to be long gone before they were up and going to work. It was St. Patrick's Day, 1964. I got up at five o'clock that morning and my dad was already up, going to work. When I said, "I'm leaving today," he said, "Where in the hell are you going?"

"I'm heading somewhere. I don't know where." So we had a few words. He said, "You know what's going to happen to you?"

"No. I don't know."

"You're going to get killed. Someone is going to kill you. You haven't done anything. You know nothing. You worked in the woods, and nobody will hire you anyway."

He was pretty pissed off that I was leaving, but he didn't try to stop me. He really gave me a going-over for wanting to go someplace else. At the time I figured he was being cruel. But he had never left Newfoundland, never gone anywhere but to the woods. And he had this idea that if you got into the big cities or someplace else where people don't know you, they might kill you or do some harm to you.

I went anyway. I left that evening on the old coastal boat, called the steamer; you had to go out by a small boat, climb up the ladder, get on board. On to Port aux Basques, then to North Sydney, where I took the train to Halifax. I was travelling alone.

I remember getting off the train right in downtown Halifax, and I was in another world. I knew I had a cousin from Conne River – Angus MacDonald – living there. My aunt had married a MacDonald. They lived somewhere on Kent Street. I wanted to find him. When a taxi came along and I said, "I want to go to Kent Street.," the driver said, "*Where* in Kent Street?" If you wanted to go somewhere, you named it – my mind was still in Conne River! He drove up and down Kent Street for a little while, and said, "If you don't know where you're going, I sure don't know." Then I remembered someone told me the name of the woman who owned the boarding house where my cousin lived. I said, "There's a Mrs. Reeves that lives on Kent Street." He said, "No problem," and took me right to her place.

When I got there, Mrs. Reeves told me Angus was out to sea and wouldn't be back for a week or so. She didn't have any space for me but to go next door. "There's a French lady there that takes in boarders, and I'm sure you could stay there." I spent probably the loneliest time in my life the next week or so watching for my cousin to come in off a fishing trawler. Every day I'd get up and go to the dock watching. After a week and a half, early one morning, I watched this fishing boat come in, and standing on its bow was my cousin.

I thought, now I got it made. I have someone to talk to. I

hadn't spoken to very many people in the time that I was in Halifax, except when I'd see the landlady, which was rarely. He came ashore, and to me he was rich. He'd got paid for his share of the fish, and he had tons of money. The first thing we did was eat. All I had was a room at the place. But no meals. I didn't eat, and I was broke and pretty hungry. He took me to this Chinese restaurant and, man, did I eat. I ate bacon and eggs and steaks. Tables full.

But I didn't get to go to work in Halifax. By this time I was starting to think, well, maybe my dad's right. Maybe no one will want to hire me. Angus had never been to any place bigger than Halifax either. After his boat trip he had lots of money, so we decided we're going to make our fortune in Toronto. "Let's go west and see what's happening up there." We took the train together from Halifax to Toronto, and I was so damn scared. We landed there in early April, and I had my seventeenth birthday there. But I damned near starved before that.

I had left home with 60 dollars that I had borrowed from my grandfather. When I got there I had only ten dollars left. We didn't know where to go to look for accommodations, so we hopped in a taxi and said, "Take us to a rooming house." The driver said, "I don't know where. All I can do is take you to a hotel."

He took us to the Edison Hotel on Yonge Street. That was no problem for my cousin. He had some money at the time, and 100 dollars then went a long way. We spent the first night in the hotel scared as hell, because it was noisy and there were cockroaches around, and we tried to figure how the hell we got into this mess. After two days, we finally found a place in a rooming house with a couple of beds, a hot plate, and stuff like that.

The next step was to find out how to get a job. That was a trial in itself. We found our way down to a Manpower building on Dundas Street. It was where everybody told us to go. "You got to go there. You got to register." Our big idea by this time was to get away from the city and get out somewhere in the country, what we're used to. So we went in with the idea that we were going to work on a farm.

Angus was older than me, so he was able to register and, almost right away, he was placed on a dude ranch. I was only 16 at the time, and my next birthday wasn't until June. They said, "Well, you're too young to be registered. You have to wait until you're 17, then come back and we'll see what we can do." Angus left that day and I had no idea where he went to. So I was stuck there with very little money. That part I didn't mind too bad. It was being left alone again. But I kept going back and pestering Manpower until I got something; I'll come back to that.

I found a little old bed-sitting room in another rooming house. It had a bed, a chair, and a hot plate and a few pots and pans. But no running water, and I didn't know where to get it from. They said, "You get hot water from the washroom." We had an outdoor toilet at home. I knew you couldn't bring water from there! I actually went down and knocked on his door. "You mean the washroom?"

And I couldn't find a place to eat. Not the kind of food that I wanted. We always had boiled foods at home, and Sunday was a special day with something cooked. 'Course, I didn't know what pork chops was. There ain't no such thing at home. And we never had chicken unless somebody killed a chicken and had it cooked. And I didn't know what pizza was or french fries. Never had those! Looking in a restaurant, I'd see people sit down and order a meal, but I didn't know what the hell they ordered. I went in one place and didn't know what to order. I saw "Tomato Sandwich" on the menu. The only tomato I ever saw was in a can, canned tomatoes. I tried to visualize what a tomato sandwich looked like. If we had tomatoes at home, it was a bowl of canned tomatoes and you ate it like that. Or, in the woods, we'd open a can, add sugar, and eat them out of the can. It was quick energy. In Toronto, I thought they'd bring a bowl and slices of bread, but it was sliced bread with tomatoes inside it!

I spent my time walking around, walking on grass wherever I could find it. If I could find some woods, I'd go in them. And I'd sit in the park in downtown Toronto. And the zoo wasn't too far away from there. I was amazed at all those tall buildings. I couldn't see anything beyond them. I remember going out at night to see the stars and the moon, get some sense of comfort, anyway. Walking along the streets I remember feeling claustrophobia. I didn't know what that meant then. But I felt like I was locked in a box and can't get out.

Walking up the street one day, I came to an armoured car. They were taking money into a bank, and this guy pulled out his gun and held it to his side. It frightened the hell out of me. I was thinking this is something they used to do. This is downtown Toronto and there was a lot of people on the street, but I was close to him and I saw him hold it to his side. I thought, "Christ, he's going to shoot me."

Going back and forth to Manpower so often, I was getting pretty hungry. One day, I was sitting in Queen's Park and this old Indian guy from northern Ontario came along with a bag full of bread. He gave me some and he showed me where all the missions were that fed people like me, where to get free dinners and free suppers. But I had to walk from Queen Street, to another mission on the west end of Toronto. It was a long walk to the table, a long walk in between. But I was in good shape, so I made my rounds. I'd get fed at one mission and go to another to get my supper. What they fed you was bare-bone stuff at the time, and if you happened to miss the mealtime, you didn't get anything at all. I still had a room and enough to pay for it, but nothing to eat.

* * *

The hardest part of all was the loss of dignity. On my way to the mission, I'd pass a great big church. And I eventually found enough courage to go in one day. When the secretary showed me in to the office where the priest was sitting, I expected good things were going to happen. I thought he'd invite me in and feed me. And right away, he said, "Well, what do you do?" I said, "Well, I cut pulp. That's the only thing I've ever done. I worked in the woods." And he said, "Well, there's not much wood to cut here. What do you want?" Finally, I told him that I was hungry and looking for something to eat. That was really hard to say.

The hardest part of all was the loss of dignity, the loss of this independent part of me that I had when I was in Newfoundland. It was what my grandfather and my father had talked about,

having the dignity to be able to take care of your-
self. Another thing that was going through my
mind was that it was Easter time at home. That's
when we feasted. We'd have huge amounts of food.
Bear meat, caribou meat, moose meat, anything.
It was a big feast for days. And here I was, stuck
in this godforsaken place, hungry and lonely. He
wasn't very pleasant, but he gave me a food
voucher for 15 dollars or so. I took it across the
street to a little grocer, and I ate for a couple of
days.

I kept going back to Manpower. They had a bunch of cubicles for interviews, and I always chose the same feller. In the end, he said, "Okay, I'll find something." Once they wanted me to go and exercise horses at the Greenway racetrack. It turned out I was too heavy. I was 150 lbs. and they needed someone 130 lbs. or lighter. Eventually they found some landscape work. The Manpower feller asked, "Have you cut grass before?" I said, "Yes." Of course, it was always with a scythe for hay. But he gave me this little push thing. I had no idea what a lawn mower was at the time!

So I spent the summer cutting grass – short little grass – for this landscaper. And he used to be amazed when he'd come to check on me, because I had all the work done. He said, "Mostly students do this and they don't work." Of course, I'd been working all my life, and pushing a lawn mover was no sweat at all, compared to what I'd been doing. And it was fun to me. I remember writing a letter to my mom, telling her what I was doing for a living and how funny it was, cutting grass for a living. In her letter back she said, "If that's what you got to do, that's what you got to do." And I tried to describe to her all the things I'd seen in the city: buildings, modern conveniences, electricity.

* * *

Working on the tracks. Some of the bosses on the railroad yelled a lot, screamed a lot. One in particular, Mike, he was Italian. He said, "You like to watch a lot." It was because I'd seen this guy with a big power saw, sawing off rails. I was fascinated by it. Rather than do the work I was supposed to, I was watching this guy. Mike asked me a couple of times to go back to work and, finally, he got mad. "If you like to watch a lot, better go someplace else." I went back to work. But to me it was all fascinating stuff. I'd never seen anything like it in my life. Even the machines, the cars, the trucks, switch-on lights, incredible meals every day. I thought I'd died and gone to heaven for a little while. It was great.

I was working in Toronto when my cousin, Angus MacDonald, and later his older brother, showed up. Angus had quit this ranch job and came back to Toronto to look for me. His brother worked on the lake boats in Ontario, and he was en route to Fort William and his boat to go out at the head of Lake Superior on the Great Lakes. We got together, bought some beer and had a big party. Everybody got drunk, and I ended up quitting my job. They talked about going to work on the railroad, and the more we drank the more we all wanted to try the railroad. Well, I wanted to get out of the city. I thought that was the best thing that could ever happen. So I had big plans to work with the railroad. That's where the big money was. The three of us marched into this railroad office looking for jobs, and we were immediately shipped out to some railroad job in the North. The next thing I knew, we're on a train heading west somewhere. West of Toronto. Free train pass and three home-cooked meals every day. Good, big meals. The work was hard, but it was more in the kind of surroundings that we liked, and we were all together.

We worked on the tracks out at Armstrong (near Lake Nipigon), and places like that up north. In Armstrong, I worked on a steel gang. And sometimes I went out on a little gas car to work. We had bunk cars and dining cars. We'd all climb into bunk cars and walk down the siding and climb into dining cars and have incredible meals.

We changed the main line rails, all manually. Everything was manual back then. There was a lot of traffic, and we didn't work a lot. We'd have to take a rail up between trains. Lift it off and put one back. Then we'd wait till the next train goes through and do it again. I loved the work. I would drive the spikes, do all the heavy work. But I got bored with it. We weren't doing enough. A lot of sitting there, waiting time, and we just couldn't do it anymore.

There were a lot of aboriginal people around Armstrong, Ontario, and one Sunday we found this empty old trapper's camp in the woods. I'd go there every chance I got and light a fire and make a cup of tea. It was a comfortable place to be away. We didn't work on Sundays, and it was a long, miserable day with nothing to do and nowhere to go.

But we didn't stay there very long. Only about a month, and we moved to another place. And soon we started to miss home, and we decided it's time to move back. I wanted to come home to try Newfoundland again. It was time to get back to the good living again, and away we went. I had left that spring and got back in early fall.

* * *

Trying to find me. To me, going away from Conne River was trying to find me. I loved the experience, the adventures, and it was the first time in my life that I didn't feel stupid doing something. I'm doing things that people said I could never do. I was taking care of me, I had a little bit of money, I was able to buy a new jacket and clothes that I wanted, and it was a new way of life. Of doing things. I was trying to find what I could do and testing my own abilities. And learning some valuable lessons along the way. It was only later that you start thinking that maybe some of the things you learned didn't help that much about what life is like.

My dad was there when I came home. He said, "Well, you made it home all right. You must have done all right. No money, of course, but at least you took care of yourself." So I stayed there for the rest of the winter. In the spring I went again, back to work with the railway, and from that I started to move around a little more. It became a migration to and from Conne River. And each trip was a little longer; pretty soon it was about two years.

But the second year away, I was on the streets in Toronto for about six months, not working much, basically no clothes, not much of anything. It was all because I had had all my gear stolen and had only the clothes I had on. It was embarrassing. By now I knew the system pretty well, where I could eat and where I could sleep. I slept in sandboxes, in old trucks, and in many other places during that six months. I was pretty down-and-out, I guess. Then this old Indian feller I met in the park took me home and fed me, had sympathy for me, and gave me some clean clothes. And, finally, I went back to the Manpower building, where the man asked me, "What are you looking for?" I said, "I want to work on a farm. I want to get away from the city." He said, "We have a job for you. It's on a mushroom farm, picking mushrooms." I had no idea what the hell they were talking about.

The farm was in Milton, Ontario. It was so good after being on the streets for six months that I stayed there for six months. I had a room. It was cleaned once every week. I had good meals three times a day. It was Portuguese cuisine, just great. I had money in the bank for the first time in my life. I had a little bit of money, although I think I was being paid about $1.25 or $1.27 an hour, not very much, but I lived right on the farm. I didn't need any money.

I also learned some other valuable trades on that farm. Like how to drive heavy equipment. For some reason or other I took to that. It was unusual, I suppose, because I never had the background. I didn't grow up with it. It was never around, and I never had a driver's licence, didn't know what it was. But I learned how to drive a dump truck, front-end loaders, and farm tractors in that six months there. I learned all those things and ended up in later years getting involved in construction and heavy equipment. So it was a good learning experience. Portuguese people worked there, too, but they didn't speak English and kept to themselves. I worked with and had become friends with some French people at the mushroom farm, and, once in a while I got to go to Milton with them. And for the first time in my life I had money. I thought, if you come from a place where you had nothing, just a little bit of something was great, I'm doing all right and should be okay now. Of course, the urge to wander a little farther came around again, and away I went.

Tractor driving on Lever Brothers Mushroom Farm, Milton, Ontario.

* * *

They used to call me the Newfoundland Tonto. My two French friends and I, we all got talking about what we wanted to do, and each one wanted to do something different. I wanted to see a ranch and how everything looked. Growing up, my grandfather gave me comic books to read. I was having a hard time learning to read in school. Maybe my grandfather knew that. I believe my fascination with cowboys and Indians came from the comic books. So we chipped in and bought a wreck of a car and drove out west together in this jalopy. The big plan was to be cowboys and finally fulfill my grandfather's fantasy, with the stetson, cowboy boots, and the whole bit.

When we landed in Calgary, the first stop was to the store that sold big hats. Then we went to the employment agency. There was no one else there. Just the three of us sitting there and looking for a job on a ranch. But no one had ranch experience and things like that. One of the guys had a truck driver's licence, so he could drive a truck, but I didn't have one at the time.

This rancher came along and, after sizing us all up, he said, "I just need two guys. I'll take those two." He only wanted the two French guys, my two buddies from the mushroom farm. Both spoke French, and I learned a little bit of French from them. He didn't want the Indian, though that was not said out loud. And, bless their souls, they said, "No, we became Indian together, and we want to work together." And, finally, he looked at me and said, "Okay, but not for very long. We'll try

Mi'sel Joe at the Calgary Stampede,
early 1960s.

On King's Ranch, High River, Alberta.

you out. The other guys are all right." I didn't necessarily want to work on a ranch, but I lasted there for six months while my friends left after only two days.

The ranch was near High River, Alberta. After the people on the ranch got to know and trust me a little more, they'd loan me a vehicle. I didn't realize that you had to earn trust; living in Conne River all my life I never fully understood that. He didn't ask me if I had a licence. But I could drive. I'd drive around, and I got to meet some people, some nasty people and some good people. One time, I was in the wrong place, at the wrong time, I got into a fight with another aboriginal fellow; he left an alley with a couple of fractured ribs. The people I hung with, who I thought were my friends, certainly drank a lot. I joined right in and I fit in with everybody else there. Downtown Calgary, in the early '60s, wasn't a very nice place, especially for aboriginal people. I certainly got a taste of racism and prejudice first-hand. They had alcohol problems then in Conne River, but not as great because nobody had money. The only booze you'd see at home would be around Christmastime, when homebrew was on the go.

I think during that time (the 1960s) everybody was just like me, probably just glad to get the hell away from reserves. I knew absolutely nothing of the Indian Act or how Indian people lived on reserves. As far as I was concerned, everybody lived like we did. Someone asked me when Newfoundland joined Confederation, and I didn't even know. It was not a part of us. Nobody came around to talk to us about Confederation, and I didn't learn anything about our Mikmaq history. I remember there was only three or four lines in the text of the grade four or five history book on how the Mi'kmaq were brought in by the French to help kill the Beothuk, which of course is totally untrue.

The people that I worked for were good people and treated me well. But I spent a lot of time by myself, like at the bunkhouse. The only times that I went in their house was for meals three times a day. I always felt a little uncomfortable; maybe it was my own hang-ups. I had my first glimpses of colour television while eating my meals there. I'd never been exposed to television. I knew it, but I never had a chance to watch it, and it bothered me that they never asked me to stay to watch the television.

After about six months there, I started to get real lonely. It probably wasn't so much being tired of the work as other reasons. Being young and silly, and getting involved with the wrong women were some of the reasons, and, of course, I missed having salt water or any kind of water around where I worked. I did meet some really good aboriginal people in Calgary. I even had an aboriginal girlfriend for a little while. It wasn't as easy to leave and head back east as I thought it would be. I started to miss the people at home, so I finally bought an old car, a 1953 Oldsmobile. By this time I had my licence, and I took the little bit of money that I had saved and headed east around November.

I don't know if I was trying to find my way back to Newfoundland or just Toronto. Even as I think back on that time in my life I didn't know what I was looking for. Driving through Regina, I was stopped by an RCMP; his first words were, "You've been drinking?" "No sir," I said. The front end of my old car was so bad I must have been all over the road. Then he saw the nine or ten quarts of oil in the back seat. "You stole that, boy!" At this stage I was starting to think this Mountie is trying to pin something on me. I tried to be calm and answer all of his questions. Finally he gave me a written warning and said, "Get this piece of junk fixed at the first garage you see." Once I got out of sight, I headed for the TCH and prayed that the police didn't catch me again.

When I reached Kenora, Ontario, I stopped to pick up a hiker, just to have someone to talk to. The car was an old manual shift. When I changed gears to stop, the gearshift broke. I could still change gears, but I had to fiddle around with it a lot. I figured, this is enough of this. I don't have good tires, and it's snowing and I still have to go around the Great Lakes. There was a junkyard close by, so I sold my first car for 15 dollars. The Great Spirit was looking after me, because the car was junk and it was late November and the weather was bad. I got on the train with just enough money to get me to Toronto and eat along the way. So I arrived in Toronto, basically broke, and I then connected with friends that I knew and moved in with them until December.

I was at the Manpower building a couple of months later, and this time they had a job for me in the North. It was with INCO in Sudbury. "We have a job for you in the mine. Do you want to work in the mine?" "Sure, it's a job." They shipped me off and I ended up going to Sudbury by train. Manpower gave me enough money to live on until I got my first paycheque, so I started my career as a miner. It was a little scary starting out, but once I got into it I really liked working at the mine. I was certainly used to hard work. The hard work there was okay, and I got along good with the crew I worked with. I was the only Indian on the shift, but there were a few other Indian people there.

It was fortunate that I always liked doing something new like that, and I can't ever remember being afraid. Sometimes I'd wonder what would happen if there were cave-ins, but I was always fascinated by how we'd get down in the mine and how it all worked once we got there. It was hard work, slogging away with the 100-pound drill eight hours every day. Of course, it was also good that I was fairly strong and a good worker.

By this time, I had been gone away from home for quite some time and I was really heavy into alcohol. Most of my free time away was spent drinking, boozing. But after awhile I got to wanting to go home again, so I started saving money until I had enough to buy a plane ticket to Gander. It was my first plane ride, and getting on the plane in Sudbury frightened me. I changed flights in Toronto and Montreal. From the time I sat in the seat until I got off, I was petrified, never got up to use the bathroom and never moved or spoke. I didn't do anything until I arrived in Gander.

* * *

I was one of those picked to go to Churchill Falls. There had been a lot of changes since I was last home. A road had been opened up from Bishop's Falls, on the Trans-Canada Highway, to Bay d'Espoir; and I was able to drive home. So I didn't have to go the whole route by train to Port aux Basques and down the coast. But I still had to get home from the other side of the river. Someone had to pick me up in a boat. They had electric lights by then, and they had old party line tele-

phones. I was able to call directly and ask them to pick me up.

This time I spent a lot of time in Conne River. I stayed and started to recover from the alcohol and all the other things I was into and began to feel good again, healthy again. I got a job with some of the companies working with Hydro development, but I got tired there and I decided to go west again. I went back, up to Toronto. Always headed there for some reason, and I went all over from there. But I always came back to the island, and then went back, away to look for work because there was nothing on the island for me.

While moving around in 1968, I learned that Manpower sponsored a three-month training course in the heavy equipment trade. When I went to Grand Falls and told them I was interested in the course, they said, "Matter of fact, there's a seat open on the first of the new year." Manpower paid my tuition, room and board at Bay St. George Community College, in Stephenville. So off I went to take the course. I got along fine with the people there and did really well.

One day supervisors from Northern Construction, the company doing the Hydro development project at Churchill Falls, showed up at the college. It was a government-sponsored project, and government was pushing for its own students from the college. We were required to wear a hard hat no matter what work we did, even if you made beds. The day they were there to watch us work, I couldn't open my locker, left the key behind. But I hoped my work impressed them and the hat didn't matter. After completing training in Stephenville, I went home, and near Christmas I learned I was picked to go to Churchill Falls as a dozer operator.

Early in 1969, Colletta and I got married. We grew up in Conne River, and went to the same school and quit at the same time. She was needed to help out around the home. The priest couldn't come to our Conne River church to perform the wedding ceremony, so we refused to go to the St. Alban's church. We compromised and got married in a little chapel in the convent. Colletta's dress and veil, and my suit and tie were borrowed from friends; the ring was borrowed from my sister. After the ceremony we drove from St. Alban's to Morrisville and reached home by boat. Our reception was at Mom's house, and the community was invited. It was an old-fashioned house wedding, with accordion music and homebrew as the main drink. People were step dancing and had a jolly old time. Twenty dollars was given to us and we used it for our wedding. Most food was brought by friends and relatives, and our wedding cake was made by Colletta's aunt.

The new job was waiting for me, and the next day I got up at five o'clock in the morning to leave for Churchill Falls for three months. I didn't last very long there. Only two months. It was to be a three-month work term, and you come out and spend 15 days at home and go back again for another three months. Although I was on a piece of machinery, I wasn't doing the kind of work that I wanted to do. They had me sitting on a D7 dozer all day, towing a roller around, and when one spread of material was rolled and done, sometimes I sat and waited four or five hours for another. I'd take my machine out, and it only took 45 minutes to spread the material, and I sat waiting again. I asked to be taken out of there and they said, "No, this is what you do." Finally, one day I was so fed up with just sitting there day after day, I said, "I think I'm going to find other work. I don't have to be here." So I came home. After getting married I realized that I had to support somebody else now. There was no work at home for men, let alone women at that time.

So I ended up going to Halifax after Christmas to look for any kind of work, and I was hired by McNamara Marine. They were building new container docks there. That's how I happened to get to go fishing. One of my cousins happened to be going to Halifax and had found work there on fishing trawlers, and he asked me, "Do you want to tag along and see what happens?" That's how I ended up on a fishing trawler in the off-season. In the spring I'd go home, then go back to operate heavy equipment with McNamara most of the summer months, then fishing again through the winter months.

A taxi driver in Halifax was sort of a contact person for the fishing company. He gathered the crew together, and I was around at the right time and right place. We fished out of Lockporte, down the east coast south of Halifax. The first time we went out on an old wooden dragger, when we came back in I hadn't earned the money back that I spent to get there. I had to go out again for ten or 13 days. It all depended on the fish. If there was a lot of fish, then ten days. If it was slow going, then longer. We fished for redfish in the Gulf, on George's Bank for haddock, and the Grand Banks for cod.

That first dragger was dirty and stank. It cracked and rolled, and I spent five days being seasick, couldn't even get in the galley. And, of course, during that five days I still had to work. It was terrible. I thought I was going to die. 'Course, it didn't help too much on that first trip out when a Frenchman from St. Pierre committed suicide. I wanted to see a little piece

40

of land; I didn't care how far off it was, I was going to get there. I was thinking, never again are you going to get me out here. Finally, I guess the old skipper figured, If I don't get this guy eating, I'm going to have to go in, and if I go in, there's no money for anyone. So he started passing crackers to me through the galley door. I could get as far as the door, and he'd pass them to me and I'd keep one down, fighting it a little more, and pretty soon I was able to eat a little bit.

But no matter how many trips I made, it never changed. I got sick when we were steaming without towing the trawl. When the trawl went over, the boat became more stable and I was all right. I could eat something. Not the greasy food. I lost a lot of weight during that time. After doing this for several years, I realized that it wasn't helping me at all. I was just being sick all the time and losing weight. I began husky and came right down to skin and bones by the time I stopped.

By then I had given up operating heavy equipment and stuck to logging operations and fishing. But I eventually got back into heavy equipment, because I was getting into supervisor's roles, being woods foreman or road foreman, which involved heavy equipment.

* * *

I wanted to be able to smell the woods again. At home I realized that, over the years, I had worked at just about every kind of job we knew about, and sometimes I'd go into the school at Conne River and talk to students about them. I talked about my work as a fisherman on ocean-going fishing

*boats, mine and factory work, work with the rail-
road, and logging, and everything they wanted to
talk about that I had done myself. In talking to the
students there, I felt like I was helping them, that
all that I had done was worth something.*

Nineteen seventy-three became my last trip away. Colletta and
our two children, Leona and Shannon, moved with me to
Sudbury that time, and we planned to buy a house there.
Conne River had little at the time. Some electricity, but not
everyone had it. And no private telephones. We considered ourselves very fortunate. We had a full-time job and we had two
kids. I got into drinking again there, but the big shocker came
when I went out to look at a house. When Colletta said, "Once
we do this, we're going to be pretty much tied to this place for
the rest of our lives." That scared the hell out of me. I wanted
to be able to smell the woods again, to walk on the bogs again,
to go hunting and trapping, and to be able to taste my mother's
cooking again. All those things called me back.

Only a month or two later, we were back in
Newfoundland with the little bit that we owned tied to the roof
of our car. There were only three or four vehicles in the community then, so I felt fortunate. But there was still no road into
Conne River. We had to leave the car on the other side of the
river.

For a long time I never wanted to go back again to anywhere. I wanted to stay in Conne River and never get involved
or do anything but enjoy the same lifestyle there. But alcohol
was around there, too, and I started to get into it really bad,
especially when my son drowned. After his death, I used that as

an excuse and I went through a hard time. I used alcohol to crush all those bad times and bad feelings. It's convenient to use things like alcohol to pretend that you've been relieved of all the burdens that seem to be on your shoulders or to blame all your problems on it. It works for a few minutes or a few hours, and then you're soon right back where you started. You forget that you have a family and that you've got a community. You forget many good things. But like a lot of people with alcohol problems do, you soon realize that it doesn't work.

I was finally able to break away from depending on alcohol, to throw it all away. But it was a struggle. After Ancelewit, our granddaughter, was born I realized that I wasn't drinking that much. I said to Colletta and the people around me that this little girl would never see me get drunk or see me take a drink any stronger than tea. To this day I have lived up to that, and I know that I'll never again drink anything stronger than tea.

* * *

I had found out how to go all around that circle.
And it's sometimes a vicious one. But I learned how to escape it and how to recover. I'd go back to Conne River and use it as a base to recover from the alcoholism and the ulcers, and all the other things that I was going through. I'd get well again to go back. Some people used to say, "Go back. Do it all over again and come back to Conne River and recover." It was always a recovery place.

That time away was not a happy one, but when I think back on it nowadays, I realize it was a great learning experience. I was able to get by in a white man's world; that was something my father said I couldn't do. I realized that I was not a bum, but that I was just passing through.

Unfortunately, a lot of people don't make it back. I was one of the fortunate ones. I knew my uncle had probably drank all his life and managed to quit for about seven or eight years. He was in his fifties when he said, "I realized for the first time in my life that the sun comes up directly in the east and it shines pretty bright." He was right. The sun is pretty bright.

And I was able to break from that cycle because I always had good teachings that I could come back to. I had something to hold on to. That was my salvation. It's unfortunate that many people don't have those teachings to come back to throughout their entire lives. I did.

And Colletta never gave up. She always knew that somewhere down the road things were going to get a lot better. And they did. She had more courage, more faith, than I did. And over our many years of marriage, we've weathered some pretty tough storms, and we came out in good shape.

Rebuilding heritage. Michael Joe, Sr. (left), and Martin Jeddore with a caribou skin canoe they built for the Newfoundland Museum.

Billy Joe, chief from 1974 to 1982. It was a time of emerging issues about Mi'kmaq identity and self-government.

2

Struggle for Dignity

The whole picture of chief came forward. After Billy Joe became chief in 1974, we started with an elected town council–type system. It was called a local improvement district. There were two offices. One was the "mayor." That was Billy Joe's role, and a few other people before that. But it was with Billy Joe, and with his appointment, around 1977, as the District Chief – that is the Traditional Chief or Saqamaw – by Donald Marshall (then Grand Chief, who was in Nova Scotia) that the whole picture of chief came forward. It was the first time since 1925, when our traditional chief, Noel Jeddore, went into exile.

AS A LOCAL improvement district, funds came from the province for medical care, collecting garbage, and so on. They were giving us about $2,000 a year. And we tried to get the province to give us some funds for whatever we needed. At the time, maybe we thought that's the only way we can do it. The Council was still pretty naive in terms of how things were being done.

Sometime prior to 1974, a petition was circulated in the community. Melvin Jeddore and Martin Jeddore went to Nova Scotia to talk to the Grand Chief about the services that were offered other Mi'kmaq people under the Indian Act. Some people in the community were upset by that and thought that they were trying to turn the community into a reserve. Ironically, most people did not realize that we were already living on a reserve. The lands in Conne River had been set aside by the old colonial government in 1870, although we were not recognized in the terms of the union in 1949 by Joey Smallwood and the federal government. When they returned, the word had already gotten back that Conne River was to be officially recognized by the federal government as a Mi'kmaq reserve.

Right away, some people in the community circulated a petition saying that, "We're not even Indians, we're Mi'kmaq." The petition was out of fear, and I understand that now. "You want people to call your kids Indians? We don't want to be a reserve. We're all right the way we are. If it were a reserve we'd be living in tarpaper shacks and living on welfare." When I wouldn't sign it, one fellow said, "You mean to tell me you want your kids to live on a reserve, live in a shack? You want people to call you dirty Indians when you go outside of Conne River?" I said, "They do that now! If anything, it's got to be better, not worse." A lot of people, maybe 90 per cent of the community, did sign that petition. And it came back to haunt us later, when we started pursuing registration to have the reserve recognized by the federal government. They told us, "Well, you people don't want it. You've already signed to that."

Billy Joe – he was my uncle – died in December 1982. He was killed in a highway accident on the way back from Milltown. He had gone there that morning to try and get welfare for a family. It's incredible that at that time the provincial government was refusing to release $800,000 that belonged to our community. If we had had that money, my uncle and Martin Jeddore might still be alive. In those early years I don't think our community realized how important it is to fight as a community. I do believe the fight with the provincial government made us all stronger and more determined to survive as an aboriginal community. Chief Billy Joe was very quiet and well-respected in Miawpukek and treated everybody with decency. He raised awareness of who we are, and he certainly knew about the traditional ways of the land, and he had some knowledge of our language. But he wasn't a public spokesperson, and it was hard to get people motivated. He never said much about many of our traditional Mi'kmaq ways, like the sweat lodge, except to say that it was used at one time and they don't use it anymore.

After his death, two names were put up for election as chief by permission of the Grand Chief: John Nick Jeddore and myself. I was surprised when I was elected, but, you know, there were still no funds going into the community, and everything was shut down. We had gone 13 months without funds, because the provincial government hadn't released the funds we were entitled to from the federal government through a five-year Federal Native Peoples of Conne River Agreement. They refused because we would not agree to them taking $60,000 of our funds for administration costs, which was never a part of the agreement.

So I took on a job that didn't pay, with a staff that was laid off because there was no money. The first thing I had to do was secure the release of funds from the provincial government. They were holding it back because we wouldn't agree to the auditing they wanted.

We started having public meetings, something not done under the previous administration. We had good people at the time who knew what we should do. Marilyn John and Jerry Wetzel, in particular, knew who to contact, how to do press releases, and all the different steps we had to take. So we made many efforts that came to nothing; the provincial and federal bureaucrats even questioned whether the "Chief" represented the community. Finally, at a public meeting I told everyone that I'd go to St. John's as the chief to demand the province release our money. And I asked people to support me and come with me.

I do not think that they fully understood or appreciated the kind of opposition that we were up against with the provincial government. We were questioned in a public meeting by some of our own band members if we were strong and smart enough to take on the provincial government. It was disheartening. But, like my dad always said, "Well, there's no sense telling you not to do it. You're going to do it anyway." I was determined. I had a feeling that this is the way things should be and that we had to keep plugging ahead, keep building.

In St. John's, we went to a meeting with the government's negotiating team and tried to convince them to release our funds and, to my amazement, they agreed to release the funds. But when we went to the bank in Grand Falls, we found that the province had called ahead and put a stop order on transferring any money. They were giving us the runaround.

So we went back to Conne River and held a second meeting and convinced about 100 people to travel to St. John's in April 1983 to petition government to release our money. Wetzel and I went to St. John's a week ahead to raise money to hire two buses for people in Conne River. Money came from church groups, trade unions, and the Assembly of First Nations. When the people left home, others were standing on the side of the road booing and making fun of them, and saying, "You're crazy. You're going to follow this crazy Mike Joe into town and take on the province." "You're not going to win anything." "You're going to come home worse than when you went in there."

So we went back to St. John's and occupied a provincial government building, the provincial minister's office in Atlantic Place, downtown St. John's. We padlocked the door inside. There were around 30 of us inside the office, including children and women. My 14-year-old daughter, Leona, was one of the children at the office. We held the office for three hours until a riot squad broke through a wall and arrested all of us, children included. I remember myself and Leona sitting by a wall when this huge police officer broke through the plasterboard wall; there were police officers everywhere dragging our people out and carrying us off to jail. When we got back to the Catholic Action Centre, you could see in people's faces what they were thinking: People at home were right. We should have stayed at home. We just came to St. John's and made fools of ourselves.

That night I looked at all this and watched people get drunk, people sitting by themselves, and a lot of them were downhearted and some cried. That's why I locked myself in a room all night and I said, "There has got to be answers." And that's when spiritualism started to happen. There were pictures of Christ all over the Action Centre, and one on the wall in this little kitchen where I locked myself in.

I didn't know how to pray. I wasn't a very churchgoing person when I was growing up, so I had forgotten the prayers. But all night I tried to pray to this picture, and every time I did that, this picture, this vision of Roddy Stevens, a Mi'kmaq person, would come. Finally, just before daybreak I said, "Well, I guess this is what I have got to do." I prayed to the vision of this face, not Jesus with the beard, but the one with the crewcut, glasses, and the round face.

I first met Roddy Stevens a little while before 1983. He was a gentle person, very sincere, from Eskasoni Reserve, Cape Breton. He was an ex-soldier and RCMP officer who was very connected to the land. His wife's grandfather was among the Conne River people who went into exile in 1925 with our traditional chief, Noel Jeddore. He spoke lots of words of wisdom and showed such respect when I met him the first time. He was older than me, a lot older, and died about ten years ago. Yet, when he met me, he took off his cap. I remember hearing that you're supposed to do that when you meet *older* people, not the other way around. But I was the chief within Conne River, and that's what he recognized. Finally, I prayed to this vision and things started to happen. So the spiritualism in my life came from that one big shock.

The next morning, after sort of getting the answers I was looking for, I suddenly realized that if we all piled in our buses and cars to go home now, we would definitely have been beaten and nothing would happen. The problems would continue, as racist attitudes, and we'd basically go home and there'd be no more Mi'kmaq. That's when I started getting people out of bed, at six o'clock in the morning! "Get up, we've got some answers. This is what we're going to do. We're going to fast until the government gives us our money." Of course, some of the people said, "No, you can't do that, because the province doesn't give a hoot one way or the other if you live or die. We'll just starve to death." I said, "That's fine, but if we don't do something, nothing is going to change at home." So they finally agreed and settled on eight people to do the fast.

We went through the whole thing. I basically told them what I had done all night, how the visions came to me and how I felt it was the right thing to do. And at our news conference we couldn't show fear. If we did, I believe we would never have gotten all the public support for our fight for justice. Show no fear whatsoever, because if it meant dying for what we believe in, then so be it. I was asked so many times during that brief, one-hour meeting early that morning, "What happens if you die?" And my answer was, "Well, if you die, then somebody else takes their place and we'll start all over again."

The commitment had to be there, whether the province withheld $800 or $800,000 from us. The principle is that, if you have something that belongs to us, to the Mi'kmaq people, it's ours. It's not so much the money itself. It's about dignity and pride, who we are.

When news media came in, of course, we had to face a camera and show that what we're saying is the way it's going to be. Maybe that was our biggest test, because any little sign that you're not serious about this will show. I guess we didn't show any signs of fear. But during those seven or eight days of fasting there was a lot of fear. Especially after seven days, when you start to get weak and hallucinate. And the emotional part of that is probably more weakening than anything as you watch all the other people going through the same thing you're going through with the same doubts. And you see in the faces of the people around you, the fear and doubts, that this is worth it. But we held firm to our decision.

The eight people fasting with me were Billy Joe, Andy Joe, Chesley Joe, Aubrey Joe, George Drew, Wilfred Drew, Mike Benoit, and Rick Jeddore. Those individuals did a great service for our community, and we should do everything in our power to never let our people forget the incredible sacrifice those brave men were willing to make.

On the seventh evening, when they brought us word that it's over, that the province had "tentatively agreed," we said to those people, "No. It's not over until we get the signed papers and cheques in our hands. Then it's over." And then we had to wait another 12 or 13 hours, until the next evening, before we finally had what we were after. It had taken time and sacrifice, but when they finally released our funds, we had a group of people in our community who believed in our-selves. That we could take charge of our own future. And things started to happen. We were more together at that point.

When we came back home from our fight with the province, my dad hugged and held on to me for a long time. And just before he let me go, he said very quietly, "Good job. I'm proud of you." When he finally let me go, both of us had tears in our eyes, and I watched him walk over to my brothers and hug them too. We were young and naive, so I don't think

"Conne River a Powder Keg. Micmac Indians talking tough"

"Funding feud continues"

"Micmac band not a government: premier"

"MICMACS ON HUNGER STRIKE"

"Goudie slams Micmac band"

"Fast to the death, if necessary . . ."

"Social Action Commission Supports Conne River Band"

"Legal advisers say Goudie within rights"

"Draft pact reached, Indian consent needed"

"Indians continue hunger strike Chief hopeful of settlement in dispute with government"

"Micmac Hunger strike: Glimmer of hope dispute may end"

"Indians end hunger strike"
"Thank God it's over!"

"Natives convicted of mischief for occupation of gov't office"

"Chief Michael Joe among them: Conne River Indians choose jail rather than pay fines"

"Advice about Fasting: Chief Michael Joe Jr., of the Conne River Micmac band, and 10 other band members get advice from Dr. John Ross, of Memorial University family medicine teaching staff, about fasting."

* * *

Local newspapers provided many reports and pictures of the clashes between the provincial government from around December 1982, through the occupation of the Minister's office and subsequent hunger strike, up until 1984, when the federal government recognized the Conne River Mi'kmaq as status Indians under the Indian Act. (In 1987 Conne River was established as a status Indian Reserve.)

Despite vigorous captions (examples opposite), newspaper coverage was generally neutral as it published strong words from the provincial government. In the caption to one photograph of band members on the fourth day of the hunger strike, Premier Peckford is reported to have said "any 'unfortunate' development that may occur will be on their own heads, and not the responsibility of this government."

Some public support was noted, but no effort was made to probe underlying issues.

* * *

we appreciated what our families were going through at home. I didn't, anyway. I can't remember my dad ever giving me a hug or telling me he loved me, but I'm sure he must have at some time.

* * *

We had to learn how to heal ourselves. After we had won the battle with the provincial government, we came back to Conne River thinking that now we could change things for the better for everyone. We expected the federal government to soon recognize Conne River as a Mi'kmaq Indian reserve, and when that happened we would have greater means to do things. Education was one of the first problems that was always on our minds. How our children were being educated, what they were being taught, needed changing. They needed to learn about being Mi'kmaq, about our own people, our language, our beliefs and culture.

The interest was there, but the Conne River school was still pretty much controlled by the Newfoundland government and the Church. The priest still controlled the school until 1985, when we finally convinced the Church to release its control over education, and they sold the property it held in Conne River to us for one dollar. It was a hard struggle in the beginning. I remember a meeting in Gander, where the priest looked at me and he said, "Suppose we release those things to you, and suppose you do have some money; what are you going to do with it? Buy cigarettes with it? You don't come here with any plans for how you're going to do all those things." It's true. We had a lot to figure out and plan for.

* * *

I had a vision experience. About a year after the walk in 1983 – I'll come to that – I had a vision experience that made me more appreciative of what I had, more sincere about what I was doing, and more respect for things around me. And definitely more respect for my own family and many other things. A day doesn't go by when I don't think about that experience and kick myself sometimes for not being totally ready for it.

It happened because we were seeking answers to a lot of things happening in the community. The spiritual people from Nova Scotia advised me on the ways to approach a vision quest. First, you have to be ready. After about a year, I figured I hadn't treated people the way I was supposed to. I'd grind my teeth when somebody said things to me that I didn't like. When I finally felt ready for my fast, I planned to do it on my grandfather's trapline.

My brother, Sului'an, and his friends Rickey and George were my helpers. The site I had picked was known as Little Island, or Little Lake. But when we got there, nobody wanted to set up a wigwam or build a sweat lodge. Everybody looked for better sites to have a vision, and every time someone said they had found one, I'd go over, look at it, and say "No. That's not the place. It doesn't *feel right*." It's hard to explain, but it didn't feel like the kind of things I was looking for.

Finally, we headed back to where my first site was and decided that's where it had to be. We set up the wigwam and cleared a place for a sweat lodge. Then we had our first sweat, and then the fast. By then it was into the second day. That night I was alone inside, alone with the fire going, when this white figure came in through the flap of the wigwam and stirred the fire with a little stick. That went on all night. Every once in a while the figure would come through the door, stare at the fire, and the flankers from the fire went up in the air. But I never saw the face.

Just before daybreak I figured, well, this is when I'm going to find out what this is all about. I want to see a face this time. But next time, when it came to the door, there was no face. It was just like a hood, a dark hole, and I looked all the way down, looking for its feet, and there were no feet. There were caribou hooves. And right away I got scared. I thought, the devil, *mindu*. It's here to get me. But it wasn't.

As soon as I realized it wasn't *mindu*, because it had kept me warm all night, it disappeared. It was just gone. And that same night I was sitting by the fire outside and I saw a pure white caribou looking at me through the woods. It was so pure white, I think even the eyes were pure white. And the antlers. Everything was white. Then that too disappeared after I realized I had seen it. I probably hadn't been so scared in my life.

At daybreak I went out and searched around the island, but there were no caribou tracks. Each time this happened I got scared and thought about all the things I had been told that I was supposed to do. My helpers were camped in a lodge half a mile away, and I later learned that that was when they became afraid to come where I was. They didn't know why they were scared, except that they couldn't walk the road. They heard things. It just wasn't a pleasant place to be.

Finally, after four days, I came out of there. We talked about what happened during the sweat lodge ceremony and prior to it. I didn't talk about the vision very much. It was important, and it wasn't important. At the time, it was something that I didn't complete, and I thought my vision quest was a failure. So we talked about other things that happened during the fast, not only to me but to them. But they didn't tell me then about being afraid to come until much later. We talked about how, when we opened the door of the sweat lodge the first time, a strange gush of cold wind came out from inside. And sitting by the fire, I felt the presence of something around me, but I don't know what it was. And every time it happened, I'd put tobacco on the fire.

During the sweat lodge ceremony, when the fast was over, we all heard people talking somewhere outside. We knew the language, but weren't able to hear them loud enough to understand. Whatever was there, that one little island was a pretty powerful place, and it was almost on my grandfather's trapline.

After coming home, I still couldn't appreciate what I had experienced. I didn't have sense enough, and I wasn't ready to take advantage of what I was searching for. I'd just had a vision, but did not follow it through. I've fasted since then, but I'm not ready for the final one yet. They say the final one is when you fast and receive the visions, and fully understand what kind of visions you are looking for and are able to talk about the spirits and, finally, get the visions in black and white, a clear understanding of the things that you are supposed to do. Then you don't have to fast anymore.

* * *

White Caribou. Although my vision of the white caribou didn't mean very much to me, two years later I decided that I wanted a Mi'kmaq name. I was tired of being called Mike or Michael or whatever. It was an English name. First, I went to Nova Scotia to find out what our clan name was. Nobody could tell me. They said the Jeddores didn't have one. The name of every animal in God's creation is used by Mi'kmaq clans. I couldn't find one for mine. So I went to somebody else who could help me select one for our family and make it our family name.

I went to visit Talking Eagle, an elder and medicine man in New Brunswick, to ask for a Mi'kmaq name. We sat around a table and he spoke in Mi'kmaq for a long time. Not to me. Not to anyone. Sometimes he'd look at the sky, and sometimes all around. Finally, he said in Mi'kmaq, "White Caribou." Then he prayed some more and talked to people around him before he said, "The name is White Caribou." It took a long time to do all this, to go through the ceremony. While he was praying, I was having visions of my own about what I wanted to be. Of course, everybody wants to be some kind of relation to the eagle. If not the eagle, then the hawk.

In the beginning I wanted to be a Screaming Eagle or Bald Eagle, or something like that. But I realize now that there are a lot people with eagle names. Sometimes they just give it themselves. But others have been passed on for generations. And they're about their experiences of survival. They're able to say, "My name is Eagle. I have been told by the spirits my name is Eagle." The ceremony went on so long that I began to worry about what Talking Eagle would say. And when he said, "White Caribou," the name didn't feel right. I didn't want to be called "caribou." I didn't want to be a dirty old caribou. That's how I saw the vision.

Maybe my expectations for the change were too high. I wanted to be something more magnificent than the caribou. We went to a sweat lodge ceremony later, and I thought I'd talk to the elders about the name during it, to tell them that I don't want that name, find me another. But during the sweat lodge ceremony, I realized I couldn't do that.

All of a sudden I recognized how many times and ways the caribou has saved our people, fed our people for thousands of years, provided clothing, medicine, and shelter, and the antlers and bones became weapons and tools. I understood the significance of the name. So it had as much magnificence as the eagle itself. After the ceremony, I walked away feeling pretty proud of myself, and it was very much part of my spiritual growth.

White Caribou is a spiritual name. It's to be used wherever and whenever. It can replace the Christian name and it can be a public name. It can be on your driver's licence if you want. With the name White Caribou, there is an explanation. Most people wonder, well, what does it mean? They have to learn about the caribou's importance to our people. Until that ceremony in New Brunswick, when it became a special name to me and I could appreciate its importance, I didn't know what happened during the four days of fasting and the visions that I had. I didn't have sense enough to talk to the spirit, the white caribou that came to help me all night.

* * *

A welfare issue. In 1984–85 I took welfare after working all my life. All my Employment Insurance was gone, and any money I had in the bank was gone. My electricity was on, but we had no telephone. But I managed to get a piece of heavy equipment and capital and put together a small logging company. I knew how to cut pulpwood!

I hired men and sold pulpwood to a contractor. In the midst of all this, somehow the welfare department in Conne River started sending me welfare. At that stage, that was great. I didn't have any money anyway. Any I was getting from the contractor I used to pay out to other people and for bills.

I remember coming home from work in the woods one Saturday afternoon. Colletta was gone to Nova Scotia and there was nobody home. A buddy of mine was living in the basement. He had no house. I remember wanting a cup of tea, but there was no tea bags, no sugar, no milk, no anything. And I opened up this envelope and there was a $120 cheque in it from the welfare department in Conne River. My first thought was to grab the cheque and go get some groceries.

I went back, poured out my hot water, and sat there

debating what to do. I wanted to visit my buddy downstairs and borrow a couple of tea bags, but I figured he was in just as bad shape as I was. Since he was working for me, I knew what he was doing.

The more I thought about it, I said to myself, "They've got me right where they want me: collecting welfare now. If I continue taking their money, I'll never survive. I'm dead." So I took a piece of paper and an envelope and I wrote a little note to them: "Thank you very much. I don't need your money." And I sent it back and never looked back. And everything has worked for me ever since.

* * *

People began to lose sight of pulling together. A lot of our strong people began to forget how important it is to try not to cause harm to their family or themselves, or anyone. It was a difficult struggle to control what was happening, so we wouldn't look like the bad guys, the way our opponents portrayed us.

Not long after I first became chief, it wasn't a good time for any of us. We were opposed from the outside – the media, government, and Mi'kmaq people on the mainland – and by people on the inside. It all put Conne River in a bad light. And I don't know if I was more angry with my opponents or the community. That was only part of our difficulties.

It was a bad time, and I'll say something about it, but first, in looking back on it, if anything, it made us all stronger, more determined. I work with those people now, and they talk about that time, what it was like in Conne River. Too many people got involved – lawyers and outsiders. After we had won the battle with the provincial government and began to achieve changes, like federal status as a reserve, our team fell apart. It's hard to explain, but maybe we lost faith in each other because we were still in a fighting mood, but burned out at the same time. And we had been too isolated from things around us, and our language and our culture were not as strong as we wanted.

Thinking back today, people who opposed me did what they had to do because they felt they were protecting the community. Information, wrong information, was there, and the only thing to do was to protect the community. If it was me on that side, I'd have done the same thing. It was lessons learned. Some were opposed to me for a lot of reasons, but the majority of these people thought it was the right thing to do. They were given inaccurate information, and along the way we were made to look like just some poor, ignorant Indians.

One of the leaders who opposed me told me a few years later that he would have done things differently. I never asked him what, but I suspect that he's had the opportunity to think through it and find a better way to sort things out between us. Some critical work was done by the opposition. It helped us to move in our favour to better understand or appreciate what happens outside Conne River. We would not have started this when we did. It would have been later. Above all, perhaps, we moved to have better communication from the Band Council. I sometimes wonder whether the troubles we had weren't the work of the Great Spirit guiding us to a new direction.

Altogether, I didn't have support for traditional ways, and, worse, the opposition did a good job in discrediting me. There were rumours over stolen money for the new house I built. These were circulating in the springtime – it was April – when seasonal work was beginning and the band did not have enough to pay people. So when people went out to tell the community, "We've got no money because the chief took all your money to build a house," people got scared. For the longest time I was mad at the community for allowing themselves to be lied to.

We were fighting the only way we knew how. The community was split in different factions and different ways of doing things. In this case, there were families fighting families. I was fortunate because all my family was supporting our traditional form of government. We were forced to take over the office space long enough to bring someone in to gain access to the computers because we had no knowledge of computers; at least I didn't.

Only after we got an accountant from Grand Falls, who found the "lost" $300,000 in an account in the bank in Grand Falls, did it become clear that I had not used Band money for my house. We never knew how the money got there. Somebody put it there. No names attached to it. But it was an orchestrated coup. We also found huge amounts of money set up in investment accounts in St. John's. Also, on the day of the coup, we got word from the bank and our lawyer that my mortgage was approved. Today, people wait over a year before getting mortgages and think nothing of it except to be frustrated. Back then, my house would have been the first CMHC house built in Conne River. Ironically, we now build many houses using CMHC loans.

Due to communication breakdown, other matters festered. People turned against us, with me being the primary target. When we gathered at my home, someone came into my driveway and slashed all our tires and hung hangman nooses at the end of the driveway. There was a complete breakdown with some of our directors and councillors. Some thought we were just a bunch of uneducated fools and nobody should listen to us. The division got so bad that we had declared our boundaries. Our opponents took over the school and Clinic for their office, while ours remained in the Band Council Building. And there was even a letter war going on between our two offices.

In 1988 a group of us went on an eight-day memorial fast in the Conne River Nutrition Centre next to the school. It was on the fifth anniversary of our successful confrontation with the provincial government. After the fast and a feast, I found out that our opponents had managed to oust the council and myself on a non-confidence vote, and we found ourselves without band funds. We called a public meeting and tried to overturn the action, but failed. Now I remained only the traditional, not administrative, chief. And Linda MacDonald, who was my executive assistant in 1988, was selected as councillor after I was pushed out. But when she tried to sit with the new council, they wouldn't allow it. They just saw her as from my camp.

With political problems like that in my community, the first thing I had to do was to inform our Grand Chief about what was happening. So I travelled back and forth to Nova Scotia and tried to build on something up there. That helped to maintain a traditional form of government in some sense. But while I was doing that, a group that pulled off the coup was in

Ottawa, advising the Minister of Indian Affairs what was happening. We were deeply divided.

The Grand Chief understood our problems. He was being challenged by non-Indian people able to take control of the Mi'kmaq government and frustrated because he couldn't do anything about it. He said, "The only thing they could do towards them is to maintain some kind of Mi'kmaq dignity and always keep each other's advice about what was happening." And we had to avoid getting involved in the verbal attacks that were taking place. It was like everybody was being attacked, calling each other names. "Keep them away from that."

One night at home I was called out of bed at two o'clock in the morning to go and talk to someone who had a loaded shotgun. I went there, and he was drunk. Alcohol abuse was creeping into people to combat things that were happening. There was a case of beer and a loaded shotgun on the table. When I asked him why he called me, he told me he wanted to go out and blast people away. I said, "Fine. Come on. We'll go in my truck." He said, "I'm not leaving without my beer," so I said, "Well, bring your beer, too."

I sat in the driver's seat, with his case of beer and his loaded shotgun between the two of us. And I started driving. I drove until daylight. We never got where he wanted to go, but by then we had talked a long time and he was feeling different. That was just one of them, people pretty much alone with their worries about what was happening to us. Other families had the same problems, but they were all isolated. Nobody came together to talk about the problems. From that came the plan to get them together doing something. So it sort of developed that we'd get together every chance we had and talk about what we could do to solve our problems. What's the best thing to do? How do we bring attention to what's happening to us? It was near the point that, if I didn't do it, somebody might end up being shot.

* * *

> *The walk. One of our first ideas was to get people moving, doing something. But they didn't want to go back in the woods to go trapping, and they didn't want to do anything within the community. It was finally decided that the 15 or 20 of us, all men, we'd walk together from Nova Scotia to Ottawa, to educate communities along the way about what was happening. It would help get attention away from the reserve and from themselves as violent and too aggressive. It would give everyone a chance to talk about things, to heal ourselves.*

So I went on down to Ottawa and to Nova Scotia, to meet with groups of people there to see if they would accept us and to organize a welcome greeting when they got off the boat in North Sydney. Of course, I advised the Grand Chief that we were planning this move and, if he approved of it, he'd have to be a part of it. He agreed and said, "I'll be with you along the way as much as I can be, and I'll also talk to other groups of people that I know who will accommodate you, feed you, and support you and do everything we can to help you."

It would be only Mi'kmaq communities in the beginning.

And if we reached Quebec, there was only one Mi'kmaq reserve en route at Restigouche, and then we'd be into Mohawk territory. But there were other contacts we could make almost all the way through Quebec, Mohawk territory, and into Ottawa. If we chose to go that far. As far as our group knew, the plan was to walk to Ottawa. But the main thing was to hope it would help people of Conne River to heal themselves.

I was already there with the President of the Union of Nova Scotia Indians and some other Mi'kmaq people that I had asked for support to greet and welcome my people to Nova Scotia, and make them feel comfortable. In some cases, it was the first time those Conne River people had been off Newfoundland island and the first time they had actually spoken to Mi'kmaq people other than their own.

On our first day of walking, it took all day to walk from Membertou Reserve at Sydney to Eskasoni, a 45-minute drive. It was quite a walk. I noticed then that people started to pair up in groups. Two people walked along and started to talk about their problems and about themselves. I thought it was pretty good. We're already talking about our problems, we're removed from the fire point and talking about ourselves, talking about our families and talking about good things to come.

By this time, someone in Conne River had faxed all the band councils in our path. It was basically a warning to chiefs and councils and people of each reserve to be very wary of Mi'sel Joe and his group of "hoodlums," because they're basically there to ask for support to take over the funds and the community to run any way they see fit. It ended by saying, "If you want to become the latest Newfie joke, then, by all means, be a part of it." The letter was being circulated in the community by the time we got there. It was probably intended to stop any support before it got started.

Just before we got to the Eskasoni Reserve, the traditional people came out to greet us and to find out what was happening. A lot of people came out. Some had this letter in their hands. But we had a mile-long motorcade. The letter had a lot to do with it. Its effect was opposite to what was intended. It showed the kind of people that we were dealing with by stooping to tell another chief and council to treat our people like crooks and criminals.

When they got off the boat in Nova Scotia, the Grand Chief had said, "Well, when you come to Eskasoni, we'll remain for the sweat lodge ceremony and a talking ceremony," and that's what happened. That night, after we wined and dined, so to speak, people in Eskasoni gave us about $1,900 to help with accommodations and food and gas. And the Grand Chief brought us all up and said, "Now it's sweat lodge time." I remember one fellow that evening talking about going to the sweat lodge ceremonies, and he asked my brother, "Do you sweat?" My brother said, "Yes, I sweat just like you. I sweat like everybody else!" This guy just looked at him.

I talked to our people later, and many of them imagined they were going to a big log house. They certainly weren't expecting a mound no more than four feet high that they had to crawl into. There were too many people, so I didn't go in right away. It was funny to watch them go in and then come out with this strange look on their face. But it was nice to hear them talk about how they felt, how their tension was gone, how they could see a lot clearer than when they started this walk.

They were talking about their families now, and wondering about the walk and what it would accomplish. And talking about how nice it was to hear the language being spoken in the sweat-house circle and to be in a community that cared, that was looking after them.

Meeting the Grand Chief, the late Donald Marshall, Sr., on the Walk.

We had come from a hostile environment at Conne River. Suddenly, we were now where people cared about us, tended to us almost like we were all that mattered on this earth. We expressed our feelings about that, talked about how nice it was to be with people that spoke the Mi'kmaq language, and how important it was that we, as a community, regain our language. And, in a sense, they realized that, if we had been speaking our own language and were strong in our own identity, our present problems would never have happened. From there, we went on to the next reserve, Whycogomaugh, where we were welcomed again. The chief greeted us, we walked into the reserve, and we were treated as dignitaries despite the same old letter that our opponents had sent ahead to warn them about us.

It had been decided that only men would be a part of the walk in the beginning and, later on, as people got tired and wanted to go back home, some of the women would come and take part in it as well. We picked them up along the way. I had a niece, Sandra Paul, who lived on the way; she had married there, and she and her little boy, Daniel, joined the walk. The baby became our mascot, everybody's buddy. Everybody who got lonely had a chance to be with him. So he was important. He was our connection to our own families. We played with him and slept with him, we nursed him, we took care of him. And being a little, small, tiny thing, he took care of us. He bridged the gaps somewhat. And it worked; the healing started to take place.

We were all on the same side, but by talking about what had happened, why it happened, and what our next steps would be, pretty soon I started to hear, "We don't have to go to Ottawa. We don't have to tell the Minister of Indian Affairs what's happening, because he already knows. The Minister is the cause of all our problems to start with." So by the time we got to Restigouche, about the second or third week, everybody agreed to go home. Everybody realized that we don't really need to go west: we had to go east. We have a problem we have to solve ourselves. So we ended our journey. Of course, we talked from time to time of going back and finishing the journey to Ottawa, but for other reasons.

I've deliberately described this conflict in Conne River as external and internal because I want to let people know that this picture they saw of Conne River around 1985 for a few years is not the real picture. I want people to see the real picture of what we're doing as an aboriginal community. And what we're trying to build. Through the years when I was no longer administrative chief, up until I was elected again in 1996, I reflected a lot on many things. In many ways, they were good years. And I felt I grew sensitive to many traditional and spiritual things.

They were terrible years not just for us, but I think for all the people in Miawpukek. The loss of honour, credibility, and respect for our community affected all of us. We have had to learn how to work together again and build our strong team just like the one that fought the province in 1983. I believe we are a healthier community today and better educated in many ways. Our memories of those terrible years will live on, but our ability to forgive is what will make this community grow and become strong and vibrant as a Mi'kmaq community.

Heritage picture. Chief Reuben Lewis, early 20th century, in the centre. To his right, Harriet Joe, a relative of Mi'sel Joe. (From J. G. Millais, *Newfoundland and its Untrodden Ways*, London: Longmans, Green, 1907.)

3

Recovering Traditional Values and Ways

The conflict I outlined in the last chapter took a toll for a long time. In some ways, those days certainly need to be talked about. It was part of our growing up. As I said, it was lessons learned. I look back at it, and we turned on ourselves. We should have paid more attention to what was happening in the community and not worry as much about what was happening on the outside; in many ways the true enemy was ourselves, all of us. Our whole administration was stressed and burnt out from our continuous fight with the federal and provincial government trying to gain recognition for our community with some semblance of dignity.

HERE I MUST SAY AGAIN that the problems we had made us all stronger, more determined to build a better community. I think I was probably sometimes arrogant in how to do things, and probably bullheaded in ways. People used that against me. I really can't blame the people in this community for being led in the wrong direction. I believe that the people in this community thought that they were protecting themselves and their children and this community. I realize now that it wasn't all their fault. I think I would have done the same thing if somebody told me "there's some money missing" or "they're stealing our money." We were failing to pay attention to our own survival, our own language, our own culture. We need to understand that more.

The walk, of course, cured a lot of people; in a sense we cured ourselves. It also helped us to think more of traditional values. We learned about the sweat lodge, and from that we looked to revitalizing many of our traditional ways, and learned more from where we came from.

* * *

The sweat lodge. *It's important that we have the sweat lodge. It's a sacred symbol of prayer and support. It's a healing ceremony for individuals and communities. It also says who we are and what we are doing. Each time we do the ceremonies, we always ask that we be forgiven for the way we do them. So we admit that we're not perfect, that we're trying to follow our traditional path as well as we can. But the main thing is that we are doing it.*

After we came back from the walk in 1988, we built a sweat lodge in Conne River. Later, some people remembered sweat lodge ceremonies in earlier times. So maybe it was done before in Newfoundland, but I think ours was the first in Conne River, and it was the first time there was ever a pipe ceremony conducted by Mi'kmaq people in Newfoundland.

The location for our first sweat lodge was made in a spiritual way. Everybody had ideas of where it should go. So we talked about this day after day and looked for the proper place to build it. One day my brother said, "I don't know if you like this spot or not." He had been standing there one day and he said, "I saw this eagle come down up the hill and down into the woods, out of sight. I wondered what the eagle was doing there. So I went over there, and it was a pretty place." He went on. "I've lived right next to this for a long time and never knew that little grassy spot was there. And the odd thing about it was that there was no eagle there. It had disappeared. He didn't come out. He didn't fly up. He must have walked off through the woods. I believe it's a perfect place for a sweat lodge." We did, too, and that's where we built our first one.

Later, we outgrew that spot, because there was too much interference from electric lights, it was too close to his house, and it was too close to the road. So my other brother decided we should look elsewhere. And the same thing happened again. Along comes the eagle again and points the way. And now we're just above the first site.

We took the sweat lodge ceremony from Eskasoni. I learned that every step in building it is a reminder of our spiritual connections and traditions. Starting from the east, how to build a sacred fire, looking for special rocks – perhaps where our grandfathers used to, but sometimes in a quarry – how to have our own mound where the pipe sits during our ceremony, where it should go and the part it plays. And so we brought back to Conne River all the steps that we went through in Nova Scotia. When people became comfortable with that, we took it to some of the other stages, like with different prayers and ways to have endurance sweat lodge ceremonies.

We basically follow one way so far. I smudge the lodge outside with sweetgrass, enter the sweat lodge first, and smudge everything inside. And I sit there for a little while and pray. I ask that we be guided through all of this, and make sure everything is as it should be, and then we bring the heated rocks in. As they come in, they're being smudged again, either with a green bough or sweetgrass. Inside, I'm doing the same thing, smudging those rocks again with the sweetgrass. When they are all in and everybody else comes in, we repeat the process of smudging with sweetgrass, close up the door, create steam with water on the rocks, and go through the ceremony inside.

Early on, we had flocks of people; everybody wanted to go to the sweat lodge. We had groups who wanted to go in, so we had a series of ceremonies. By the end of six months or so, that one sweat lodge was ready to be put out to pasture again. One of my first thoughts was not to have non-Indian people involved in the sweat lodge, but I had an elder in Nova Scotia tell me, "No, no, you don't do that. You bring as many people as you can. You're trying to survive, you're trying to educate other people, and you just can't explain it. It has to include and be done by other people." But people must come with a good attitude: "I'm going to learn something from this, and I have a positive feeling that this is something new." I've had a sweat lodge ceremony where I've been burned, my ears burned, my shoulders burned, when other people who sit next to me say, "Gee, it's cold, really uncomfortable." The only explanation is that sometimes that happens with a positive force or really bad negative force. But being a conductor of a sweat lodge ceremony, sometimes you take on an extra burden of trying to keep all this together and really put more concentration in keeping the negative force out and the positive force in.

We all need something to lean on, something to believe in. If the Church hasn't helped, and the treatment centres haven't done it, then there are spiritual connections. The sweat lodge is where you can talk openly about how you feel about alcoholism, family abuse, or whatever. It becomes an important support. And, if you get to the point where you want to go back, you know there will always be people in the circle who do care about me, and do care if I survive or not, and do care for my family. And, too, I've heard a lot of talk from older people on how it helps not only the spiritual part, but also aches and pains. It's one of the best medicines for stress.

In many ways the sweat lodge has helped us all to be happy again. It has helped to foster interest in all our traditional values and ways.

* * *

Ceremonies. *Spiritual treatment for me is more of an invitation to participate in something that's unique and special to Mik'maq people in Newfoundland. It's part of our system that helps you deal with everyday life. The sweat lodge ceremony is a spiritual time. It is a way we find that helps to bring young and old together, to talk about alcoholism, to talk about family abuse.*

I think basically you can heal anything you want in a sweat lodge ceremony if the people in the sweat lodge are in tune with each other. Of course, it won't happen if there are so many different minds going in different directions. It takes a lot of practice, a lot of sitting down together to get this right. We help by calling on the spirits from the four sacred directions.

One ceremony that we do every time we meet in any formal way is the sweetgrass ceremony. It is a purification ceremony. It goes with smudging when the smoke from the sweetgrass is wafted over one's body as an act to cleanse the spirit. The purpose of the ceremony is to ask each other to have respect for each other, to care about each other, and if we argue or disagree within say a four- or five-hour meeting, that we don't take it out through the door and take it home, that we leave it within the building and that we don't leave as enemies.

There are many other traditional ceremonies, some coming back. The give-away ceremony is one when you give away something that you value. It breaks the cycle of the mind. I learned about it when a chief gave me a medallion made by his grandmother; it has beads on it over 100 years old. It can be done at an early age. It is thoughtful for a family to get involved, particularly with younger kids. To give away a favourite doll or teddy bear, things like that.

Many of our ceremonies help with healing, but we are also interested in what you can call "remote treatment centres." It's more of a traditional system on the country where you learn to build wigwams, you learn to trap, you learn to survive off the land. You take people out of an unhealthy environment and put them back in a traditional setting and help them to heal themselves.

* * *

Sentencing circles. After we brought the sweat lodge to Conne River, the sentencing circle came in through the help of Judge Robert Fowler. We started calling the sentencing circle a healing circle, because that seemed more appropriate. We did have informal circles before that, where individuals could express openly their concerns and worries when it was their turn to hold the "talking stick," or perhaps an eagle feather, that goes round the circle.

The sentencing circle started a few years ago. It's a community justice process for young people who got into trouble. It's really a sentencing and healing circle all in one.

When it's a serious offence, the court deals with it. The sentencing circle is more for problems like vandalism. The case is first given to the court worker to examine; they'll either say "yes" or "no" to dealing with it. If they think it's something we can't handle, they'll send it back to the courts. Even when the young person asks to be judged by our sentencing circle, it's not always accepted. It has been working really well. We've had cases where a young person broke some school windows, and after the sentencing circle, that person never ever offended again. It has a really good record in that regard. Much better than the courts, anyway.

The difference is, if you go to court, you get chastised by the judge. In the sentencing circle, you get chastised by the community. But it's not so much chastising as sitting with a young person and trying to find out why he or she is doing what they're doing.

When it first started, some offenders thought it would be smooth sailing to go through our circle, rather than face the court. But it's much harsher than a court, because you have to face people in the community that you offended. Those people are invited to that circle, and offenders have to explain why they chose to offend somebody that way. And then, when the sentence is handed down, it could be that he or she has to work with that person for six months, or a year. And reports go back to the sentencing circle, which reports back to the provincial court.

* * *

The Mi'kmaq always had a seasonal routine. When we think about our traditional ways, we think of the seasons. Hunting and trapping – for caribou, bear, beaver, otter, rabbit and so on in the fall and winter, and fishing for salmon, eel, and so on in the summer. Living on the land remains in our blood. Unfortunately, there is much I don't remember about how it was practiced. I probably had no appreciation of what my grandfather did, but it was certainly respect for the animals; I've seen my father do it.

Today, some people think that sort of respect has gone, but perhaps it is finding its way back again. Like, when a beaver is killed crossing a road, more of our people think of moving it back, putting it in the river again, where it came from. Never leave it on the road. I don't know where that comes from, but people do it. I've done it. There's some connection there, some respect.

In 2008, I got the province to place an island – Eagle Island in the middle of a lake, or pond, as we call it – under protected status. It doesn't have a place on the map, but it'll be known as a protected site. We take the bodies of eagles there, after we have taken the feathers that we need for ceremonies. Long before this, I had the written agreement out of Rex Gibbons, when he was minister a long time ago. It says, any dead eagles turned in to the province through the course of Wildlife, they will send them on to us. They're still holding up to that at this time.

It's important to hold onto our traditional values and culture. So we encourage our people in crafts, and hunting and trapping. Back in the '70s, our band organized a trappers' association, and federal-provincial money helped us supply trapping gear to those who wanted to go trapping. Elders and more experienced members helped the younger ones, men and women, learn about the traditional ways, customs, and territories. They shared their knowledge and skills.

Trapping is only seasonal and a small part of our economy, but we've run programs to train anyone who is interested in them – like the trapper incentive program that supported them for a month to go out on the land, and we even managed to buy their furs. But there wasn't always money to run the program, and you weren't just free to hunt and trap like in my grandfather's time. You have to be licenced and obey gov-

The photograph of two guides (c. 1907) with caribou antlers strapped to their traditional "bundles" has become a favoured "heritage" picture, symbolic of the Mi'kmaq hunting tradition. It first appeared in J. G. Millais, *Newfoundland and its Untrodden Ways* (1907) with the caption: "Micmac Indian Packing. John Hinx and Steve Bernard."

ATVs. Today's vehicles for hunting.

ernment rules, the animals aren't always where you could go, so you couldn't know what money would come from it. Some families that started trapping for the first time are still at it. But it's up to the individual, everybody who wants to can do it. So we still trap.

Classes on trapping and preparing skins.

* * *

Women were powerful in the everyday life of the community. There was an old lady they called Kitty Burke. I don't know what her real name was. People across the bay from St. Alban's – they would come through in the fall to go down to

Little River to cut logs – when they passed through Conne River they would all stop to visit her. She was a medicine woman. We used to call her n'me in Mi'kmaq. It doesn't mean mother or grand-mother. It's someone that you hold in high regard. She was the one that would show up when someone was sick.

When I was young, not so young that I can't remember, I was very proud and a little afraid of Kitty Burke. She was telling mother, "This is my man here, I've come to see him." It was me she was talking about. And every time she would come to see me, she would bring gifts for me. Berries or cookies or something she had saved. I wasn't related to her in any way. Maybe she saw something in me that she didn't see in other kids, but the other thing was, every time she saw me, it didn't matter where it was, she would kiss me. My mom would say, "Your girlfriend is here."

I remember when she died, I was still quite young, Mom insisted that I go to the wake at her house. She also insisted that I give her a kiss. I remember the feeling of how she felt so different, and that bothered me for years. I wondered why I was forced to do those things, but I think it was out of respect for this lady that paid so much attention to me when I was younger. A lot of people feared her, there were lots of stories of her power, but she made medicines for people who needed them.

The clan you belong to comes from the mother, the boss, not the father. I mentioned earlier that the different parts of the community were along the lines of a clan and that each one had eight or ten families. In our case, it was our grandmother on both sides. But if there's a break, like my great-grandmother, who married a non-aboriginal, you would adopt the next clan closest to your great-grandmother. So you always had a spirit guide. Everyone in a clan has the same spirit guide and spirit animal protector. We identified a clan symbol by its unique symbol. I'm in the bear clan. That means I don't eat bear meat, I don't hunt bear, but I can use it for medicine. The bear is our spirit guide.

Women were powerful in many ways. There was about a half a dozen *n'me*, older women, doctoring, looking after people and things like that. The last one was probably in the early 1950s and '60s. And there was one man, *n'me-tay*. We never thought what they did was magic. Like Mary Lewis. She was such a gentle soul, but powerful in her own way, and our own people would be afraid of her. Like the story about when my dad and a bunch of people had a few beers – homebrew – at our house around Christmastime, and her grandson got sick and they took him home. When they went in the house, my dad heard her from downstairs and threw the poor guy in and left in a great hurry! Dad talked of her many times, and I'm old enough to remember her. She would come to our house and bring me dogwood berries and cream cracker biscuits. Mom made us go to see her when she died. I didn't want to go, but I had to, it was respect for her.

Some stories about the *n'me* come from across the bay. One, a Mi'kmaq lady, lived where some people gave her a hard time. In one story, she said that the boat that they came in on wouldn't be able to leave the bay again until they had apologized or did something nice for her. Ice came in the bay and the boat couldn't leave, and all kinds of things happened. Whether the stories were true or not, there was this fear among some of our older Mi'kmaq people that they could cast a spell on you, and to some extent the fear is still there.

Someone like that, with that power, was called the devil – *mindu* in Mi'kmaq. That story is from before when the missionaries showed up. But the devil was a good person in Mi'kmaq. It was the missionaries who changed him into something evil, and when someone was bad that way, they automatically became *mindu*, the devil, or *manitou. Manitou* is somehow mixed in there, too. I've heard it used. But m*anitou*, as I understand it, is also a good spirit.

Now some women, like Harriet Joe, sister of Reuben Lewis, who was the first chief, and my great-grandmother on my father's side, were in a sense medicine women. She was the midwife not only for Conne River, but for the whole district. It wasn't uncommon for her to be out during the night, or away two or three weeks. As a baby was born, she would move on to the next household. And she made medicine for the people who needed it. She cared for the family; she was the person who made medicine for my dad. Cough medicine, with the cherry bark, and the Vicks and the molasses.

Now my grandmother on my dad's side, Amelia Joe, she was the last midwife up until around 1960. I talked about her earlier. She told us about a baby who looked stillborn. She moved the little one to one side while she tended to the mother, but later, on going back to the room, discovered the little one was still alive. And she wrapped it in cotton and, as she said, "I put it in my bosom." Next to her skin, the baby became warm and when it was lively enough she put it in a shoe box in the oven door to get heat from the oven. And the little one grew up but he wasn't a giant of a man.

Amelia taught my aunt Molly (Dad's sister) to be a midwife, but that fell apart with government regulations and doctors telling women to go the hospitals, so midwives were done away with in Newfoundland. Women had to go to hospital in Harbour Breton or Grand Falls, sometimes well ahead of time, to wait for the birth; they stayed in boarding homes or with family. There are many stories of harrowing journeys getting to hospital – a lot of babies were born on the highway – and bringing the baby back home. Aunt Molly helped out in an emergency, but the change was difficult.

There were some people in the community who we believed to have magical powers. We grew up with stories that they could cast spells, and you didn't mess with them. People were afraid of them. If you crossed them in any ill way, they'd cast a spell on you. Everyone had to be nice to them.

We grew up hearing stories about how some of our older people dealt with racism and prejudice in their own way, like the time an older gentleman from Conne River showed up at a store in a little place called Gaultois. It was two days away from Conne River, going by rowboat. You had to take your furs there, and you went there to get provisions. It had the nearest grocery store. One time the man took some furs into the store to have them graded, but the fellow who graded them wouldn't give him the price that he wanted. He felt he had been robbed.

The story goes that he told this fellow, "That's okay. You robbed me now, and you can see my furs. But next year I'll be back and you won't be able to do that, because you won't be able to see the furs." And on his next trip back to Gaultois the following year, this fellow was blind. So he couldn't see and he couldn't rob him or anyone else again. Stories like that are kept within the community, sometimes by people keeping notes. They're not published or anything like that. All these happenings are now stories, but they connect us to the past, even as we have mostly lost our belief in magic.

Women today are involved in any number of ways in our community, but some visibly carry on our traditional crafts – baskets, moccasins, jewellery, dream catchers, the list is too long to give here – and traditions such as shawl dancing.

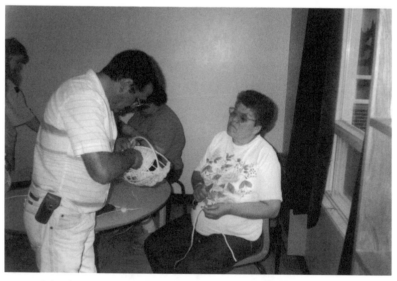

A basket making class; revitalizing a craft tradition. c. 1996.

* * *

Lots of our history is connected to Miquelon. *If you go back to 1800, Mi'kmaq people were going*

out to Miquelon for burials, marriages, and bap-
tisms. It includes some of our people getting
caught and dying from landslides when they
stayed close to land as they went up and down the
coast by canoe on the way to Miquelon.

In Conne River, a brand new church was built a few years ago. It replaced the one built in 1905, but there was an even earlier one over in the cemetery. It may have doubled as a schoolhouse. When we went out to Miquelon, we found the church there was identical to the one we had had in Conne River. The one in Miquelon preserved all the French things about the church, and it's a sin that we tore down the one in Conne River. It cannot come back.

It wasn't until around the early 1900s that a priest was sent into St. Alban's; that's three miles across the bay. And he came down to Conne River once or twice a year. Now he comes down at least once a week. Mind you, not that many people are in church, but he still comes down. I mentioned earlier that, when I was growing up, the priest would come down on St. Anne's Day. He'd come down for a week or so at other times and usually stayed in the priest's quarters in the school. Some traditions have thankfully gone. I remember that time, because we stayed off the road. We didn't want to meet the priest; if you met him, you had to kneel down, maybe on rocks, whatever was there. You had no choice. You had to kneel down in the road and wait for the priest to pass. And take off your cap, if you were wearing one. Didn't matter if there was a hole full of water, you went down on your knees until he passed.

And the priest, in my time, was the "nurse" and the "dentist." My mom and dad, if they had to have teeth pulled, they went to see the priest, and a lot of times he didn't have any cocaine. My mom had all of her teeth removed without that. So did my dad. I even went to him one time. I had a toothache. I crossed the bay in the middle of winter on the bay hike, and I asked him to pull one of my teeth, but he wouldn't do it. He said I'd better go see the doctor.

It is important to us that our Mi'kmaq prayer book has been restored and returned to our community. That was in June 2000. It had a long journey, and it connects us to the many people who touched it over nearly 200 years. It was written when our people were still writing, reading, and talking in our language, expressing our culture and our identity. The script shows the symbols our people often used to record our own history. I believe, as it's in our own language, our elders prayed for the things that they themselves felt they needed to say to the Great Spirit, not necessarily what that priest wanted them to say. It links us to a way of life that has all but vanished. For generations the book was felt to hold spiritual power that could be called upon to cure sickness and ward off evil.

We want the Mi'kmaq prayer book to encourage our elders to teach our history, its lessons, about our fears and experience with the Churches and governments, and the traditions we have lost and those we held onto or are reviving. And we hope its very existence ignites interest in our young children to know more about their own history and culture.

The old church (St. Anne's) at Conne River, early 1900s. The sign above the porch door, in Mi'kmaq language, states: "No spitting of tobacco juice on the church floor." Mi'sel Joe's grandfather is on the far right.

Matteau and Uncle Mick in front of the statue of St. Anne (c. 1950s). The Saqamaw's medal was hung on its neck after Saqamaw (Noel Jeddore) was forced into exile in 1924; it remained there until sometime when Billy Joe was acknowledged as Saqamaw from 1974–1982.

The rebuilt church photographed in 1998.

* * *

There are still wakes, wakes at home. In these we try to maintain four days of mourning – four suns. And on the fourth day you can be buried. People are more conscious of that now than ten or 15 years ago. I've often heard: "We got to wait for four suns."

Older ladies in the community – a sort of church committee – used to make a shroud when people died, to wrap and place over the face. They were all embroidered around the edges. And there were also coffin makers in the community; a lot of older people had coffins or some boards for their coffin stored away in their loft or shed for when they died. So, if they died

94

and it was in the middle of winter, you didn't have to go looking for boards. You just took down their boards and made a coffin. And, generally, people that made the coffin would make the cross for the cemetery. They'd carve into it the names, dates of birth and death. But all that stopped many years ago.

Nowadays people will ask for more of a Mi'kmaq ceremony with drums. And we do eulogies for people that want them. But before it was never accepted in the Church. You were never allowed to do that. And people want drumming or Mi'kmaq songs at the cemetery. So there's a mixing of the two together now, which is great. I just wrote a letter to the priest, acknowledging his part in the mixing of the two.

We see the wake as a healing process, where everybody gathers with the family and stays with them 24 hours a day. Four days. And food is definitely part of that. People bring lots of food. And during that time in Conne River, you would have time for tears, time for jokes and laughter. And everybody will talk about the person that's passed. What he's done, the funny things he's done, the funny things we all do. And you probably spend a couple hours laughing and talking, and all of a sudden you start crying, everybody is crying.

So you go through that for four days, and that's an important part of a community healing. Not just individuals. And the Band Council acknowledges someone passing by closing our office for half a day. And for the funeral everything closes down for the morning. We're still acknowledging some of the old ways that's been around. That's part of the community. There is much to learn.

Unfortunately, not everyone understands our ways. When my uncle died, I wanted to talk to the doctor about our belief that when you die, you go to the spirit world, and that you should go to the spirit world as you were when you were born. We want to make sure that anything removed during an autopsy was all put back and in place. He didn't take any time to talk about my concern. He sort of ushered me out, and we ended up having this discussion in a lobby. He had no concern of what I was talking about, or wanted to talk about, except to say that "when we cut it out we put it back."

* * *

In so many ways, we were no different from other Newfoundland communities. We had mummering, pretty much the same as in the outports. People dressed up and disguised themselves and went around to people's houses. And in the schools, they had a time when we dressed up and came to school in costumes along the lines of the mummering. Sometimes that was at Christmas or just after.

In many ways, we did things like other Newfoundland communities. During Christmastime, everybody had a day. Like Johns' day would be for all the Johns in the community. Twelve days, and everybody had a day. And each evening, we would all go visit the Johns. And they would sing and hit the side of their skin boots and sing a little Mi'kmaq song, "Quay, Quay, Quay," and then someone would invite them in. And there was a ceremony with a piece of wood in the stove. You put it in the stove, take it out, and put it away until next year. The piece of wood was shaved down, it had curls on the end – it would curl up, and that's what they would leave behind. Plus that junk was burned and put up overhead somewhere until the next year. I never saw it, but we were doing it in my father's time and my mother's time.

Of course, the one unique thing about us is that we now speak English, or are trying to, because Mi'kmaq was outlawed. We were already doings things our way, had our own language, our own culture and identity, until the Churches and governments outlawed much of our way of life after the first Mi'kmaq was baptized in 1610.

* * *

Stories of Mount Sylvester. *We also have stories of little people. As soon as we were old enough to move around and understand what was being said you heard about "little people." There were stories told on nights when everybody had no other entertainment except for storytelling. People would talk about the little people that they had seen or someone had seen, and they knew the little people lived on Mount Sylvester. It was named after the Mi'kmaq guide Sylvester Joe, who guided William Cormack in his 1822 exploration of the Newfoundland Interior.**

---

* Although some historians follow the name that Cormack used for his guide across Newfoundland, namely Joseph Sylvester or Silvester, many authorities such as the *Dictionary of Canadian Biography* accept Sylvester Joe.

I did a fast on Mount Sylvester around 2003. I hoped to get a sense of how Sylvester Joe felt and how he thought about the mountain named after him by William Cormack, a non-native person, although the mountain was on Mi'kmaq territory. And I wanted to understand about the little people. Mount Sylvester is definitely a special place, a sacred place.

There's a cave on Mount Sylvester and a big lake below the mountain. You can land a seaplane there and walk up. It has a straight face on the south side and a long slope on the north side. Old Mi'kmaq people used to describe the difference between the north and the south sides. They'd say, "If you lost your cap over the south side, it would be a day's walk to go and get it."

People would go there and leave gifts – tobacco, food, cloth, things like that – generally in the summertime or fall. But they wouldn't go down into the cave. And they'd say, "Don't take your children to the cave." They feared some harm would come to them. The belief is still there, that you shouldn't take children to the mountain. But just recently, George Drew, one of the fasters with me in 1983, had his little granddaughter there and she is all right, so perhaps that idea is being put aside.

And there are stories of an old Mi'kmaq trapper who was pretty down-and-out in his life until the little people showed up to take care of him. One fellow, who died about 1974, used to tell the story about how the little people would come into his camp and spend days and days with him. When asked to describe them, he said, "They were just little people. Didn't look any different than me or you. They had their chiefs and people that came under him."

I don't know whether those stories are all true or just imagination. I know one gets glimpses of little people – fleeting sightings, like a shadow – after a purification, a four-days fast that frees the body of impurities. And I know that gifts have been left there for a long time. If you were to treat them wrong or not show them proper respect, then they might become the *mindu*.

Gifts came from people asking for protection, peace. Leave me alone. I'm not bothering you. I respect you and I've given you a peace offering, so that we are allowed to go out and use the land without being bothered by little people. You treat the little people like any other person. If the little people had one place and you knew that they were there, then you put the offerings there. They were there, and you stayed well within your own boundaries. I've heard Newfoundlanders, too, believed in the little people.

* * *

If you want a cure from anything that bothered you, Bay Nord was the place to go. I had heard about it all my life, about magical cures. You go there, leave offerings, drink the water and leave. And people take some of the Bay Nord water back with them. My mother and father, and even my grandmother, they all talked about it. So to me it was a natural place to go, to wash in the water, to drink the water, to see the gifts left all around underneath the rocks, walking sticks and so on.

I made my first trip there in 1976. My uncle Gabriel had told me about all the people who used to go to Bay Nord, like his sister, Teresa. She was born with cataracts or something over her eyes and she couldn't see. He told me how he took her there, stayed for two weeks or so, camping around the mountain. And he washed her face and eyes every day in the water. Before they left there, she could see. She died with cancer back in 1979.

I had been bothered by ulcers for a long time by then, and I was still drinking. It was one of the things I got into after getting away from Conne River and into french fries and all those things that I thought were delicious but made my stomach sick. It was giving me a hard time and got to be so terrible that I went to a doctor. The doctor said it was ulcers. So it was, "Drink some medicine, take some pills."

But the ulcers were still bothering me so bad that one day I said, "Well, there's only one thing to do." I went and got my uncle, and we spent three days at Bay Nord. We drank the water from Cross Brook, a little stream near the Cross, said our prayers, left our offering, and came down. It's a hard walk in the healthiest of conditions. I still drank after that, but the ulcers didn't bother me. And I didn't have to take any more medication.

Uncle Gabriel had lived with us at one time when we were growing up. He was probably a poor role model, because he was always drinking. Whenever we got together, we were probably more like drinking buddies. But on the day that we went to Bay Nord, there was no mention of taking alcohol. And none was taken along. And there was absolutely none there at all. Although I was drinking every other time, it just happened that way. And he was probably worse off than I was. He came right off a big bender the morning I got him. I don't know if he'd want to get into thinking on what we were doing.

My father had told me stories he remembered about people going there to be cured of one illness or another, and about coming out of it cured. Walter John was one of them. He went back there year after year for the water and kept himself going for 25 years or so. Over those years he died in the hospital a dozen times! In one story, he was at the Health Sciences Centre in St. John's, and Walter said, "I was actually put aside and fit for death. The living dead. I was just lying there day after day and I couldn't help myself, and people had to take care of me like a little kid. They were feeding me just Jell-O and ice cream, until one day they put me near a window. The sun was shining. So I had a long talk with myself. I decided there was things I could do. I don't have to take this kind of stuff." And "If I ever get strength enough to get out of here, I'm going to Bay Nord, drink the water and cure myself, like my father and all the people had done before." He asked to see the doctor, and told him, "I want some food. No more Jell-O and ice cream. I want food I can chew." People from home brought him solid food, like beaver and caribou, and he got better. And as soon as he got his strength back, his first trip was to Bay Nord.

Within a year, he had such energy that, on one occasion, even the young people complained about him. In the early 1980s, we hired him as a guide instructor, a band instructor. The one complaint from all the young people who worked with him was that they couldn't keep up with Walter. He finally died a little while ago.

It is a sacred place, but some people have gone there to rob gifts, especially once helicopter pilots found the place. The old coins that were left there, mostly gold, silver, disappeared. There was a saying that if Mi'kmaq people went there and tried to leave with any of the gifts, they would never get down the mountain. There was some force that would draw you back. The brother of a friend of mine went there and he tried to take some money. His story is that he had to put the money back. He couldn't get down the mountain, no matter how hard he tried; he just never had the energy to leave. Another thing that happens when you are going there, when you arrive and climb up it's pretty rugged, but when you get up there you get this enormous feeling of energy, very light. I find that when I reach the bog area I'm running, like I'm bouncing, defying the law of gravity.

The Mi'kmaq in Nova Scotia have something similar in Glooscap Cave. When I met with Mi'kmaq people there we talked about little people and about having the same types of beliefs. And I was told, ever since I was young, that Glooscap Cave is pretty much the same as what happens now with the Cross on Bay Nord.

* * *

For everyday things people used the plants we have. But one of the traditions we have generally lost is our knowledge of plants.

We have been trying to teach people about our healing plants, and we have a "traditional walk" where some of them can be found. We continue to develop the trail, and it's quite a walk to go all the way, mostly along the Conne River. We are still in the

Birchbark wigwam on the Medicine Trail.

process of identifying all the plants and tagging them. There's many plants we'd like to study, like beaver root for when you get in trouble with your water. I have used alder leaves; they're good for a headache. You can put them on the forehead under a baseball cap or by tying a rag around them.

One of the old-time favourite medicines is "Seven Sorts" – it's like molasses. Put it on a cloth, like a plaster, for cuts, and aches and pains. But I've also used it, a tea of the ingredients, in the sweat lodge ceremony in a spiritual way by putting it on the hot rocks to become part of the steam. It helps to link with the traditional healing of the past. And sometimes I use a tea of blueberry leaves.

Seven Sorts seems to be magical; if the pain moves, then the Seven Sorts follows the pain. I found out the ingredients from elders: barks of cherry, alder, and dogwood; the roots of yellow root and beaver root; the entire boughs of ground juniper; and the tips of the balsam. All are boiled together and the solid pieces removed. To make it for a medicine, the remaining liquid is boiled down to the thickness of molasses.

And, of course, we always tell people about the importance of good nutrition. Mother had a really tough time when growing up; her mother and her two sisters died of tuberculosis. She took care of them, but she never ever got the disease. It was highly contagious back then. I understand from my mother and father, they had lots of greens and their own berries, and they had their own gardens and encouraged us to eat off the land in the summer months. We didn't realize it then, but that's what it was doing, keeping us well.

And we would eat the leaves from the blueberries. We're just finding out now that it's a powerful medicine. And we'd chew the tops off the small spruce trees in late June and the early part of July. And go along the bogs, take up the ferns, a banana-type fruit, and we'd eat that. And, of course, we always had lots of potatoes and turnips in our root cellar during the winter months; Father would put a cat in there sometimes, because the rats would get in. We all loved good eating, and fresh meat for the cat!

* * *

We need to let people know about the things that we are doing, like building drums and canoes. The more people I tell about us, not just the Mi'kmaq people in Conne River, but the Native Canadians, increases our chances of survival.

We have made a number of drums since our walk. The year after we were back, we made our first one and went up to the church on St. Anne's Day. We set up behind the church door and started playing. Some naysayers soon came by and had a good chuckle over us. But when the priest came out, he wanted to talk to us; he invited us inside the church, and we realized that we are doing something right. People who stand back and laugh at it, maybe they're afraid. Afraid of themselves. We made it more to see if people would accept it. I had never had a drum in my lifetime, or had my father. To have our own drum would be the revival, the start of something, so we made a drum and showed it in the school. I don't think it was well-accepted, but some think it was. And when this whole political thing started, we gave the drum to the museum, now the provincial museum at The Rooms, in St. John's.

Drummers, choir, and dancers of Conne River (1990s).

Drummers chanting (c. 2000).

Nowadays the Church has come a long way in being more accepting of our own beliefs and spiritualism, particularly around sweetgrass ceremonies and Mi'kmaq songs that we sing in church. We're no longer afraid of the Church or the priest. And we accept them as part of the community and our own growth. Part of that is many fine drummers, young and old, that we have. I'll mention our CD with drummers and choir later.

In 1983 I visited Alberta, where I learned that a Mi'kmaq canoe built by our people was on exhibit at Calgary's Glenbow Museum. At the time, leaders of many tribes were attacking the Glenbow Museum and others in Canada for possessing and displaying sacred Native relics as if they were just "things" that meant nothing special to anyone. I couldn't see the canoe at the time, but I kept thinking about it. It was made by our Mi'kmaq people, and it said something to me about when and how our people first crossed the Gulf of St. Lawrence from Nova Scotia to the island of Newfoundland. We believe our people went back and forth long before the Europeans arrived. The canoe is proof of my people on the land then. When I thought about this, the idea grew that something similar needs to be done in the present.

While I was away in Alberta, my political opponents used the information that I was visiting the Glenbow Museum to see the canoe to discredit me. But the idea and potential of the canoe persisted in my thoughts and among my supporters. I went back to Alberta the next summer to see the canoe. Seeing it was like touching a fork to an electrical outlet. All kinds of things were happening. My mind was going a thousand miles an hour, thinking about the things we could do. Like raise awareness by taking this canoe out of the museum, if I could get my hands on it. But that was impossible. And it would have been crazy to try to steal the canoe from the museum! We had to raise our awareness in other ways. Let's build our own canoe.

When I got back to Conne River, we sat night after night talking about things we needed to do. The canoe project always came up in our discussions of what we were going to do, but, over the years, it was one of the projects that sometimes sat away in the fog. Until something came along to spark the dream again, that we should get back at it. And the more we talked about it, the more we realized that it wasn't just a dream, just a canoe.

In March 1995, I visited Maui, in Hawaii, with two friends from Memorial University, in St. John's. The three of us were invited to go there to meet with aboriginal people involved in preserving and renewing the aboriginal Hawaiian traditional culture. I especially remember the traditional healer, the boat builder, and the men involved with building a traditional Hawaiian double-hulled sailing canoe. We joined the Hawaiian crew on a trial row and sailed along the

A Hawaiian double-hulled canoe preparing for a trial voyage in 1995. Mi'sel Joe stands toward the right.

coast. It was as if the canoe was alive, flying over the warm Pacific sea in the company of humpback whales. What we learned from the Hawaiians about their canoe's spiritual importance strengthened my ideas about our own Mi'kmaq canoe. Later, we spent nearly a week with the Maui healer, who privately taught us about his traditional healing knowledge and beliefs, and we visited the community herb/vegetable garden.

Like the people in Maui, we realized that the boat was pretty much a spiritual craft. It carried and connected them to the spirits of their ancient people. When I got home to Conne River, we had already developed plans for our canoe, but now pretty clear thoughts about the canoe bringing almost magical power came to us every time we spoke about it.

In April 1996, my university friends and I travelled again together, this time to England. Our purpose was to make presentations about traditional ways among our Conne River, Mi'kmaq, people. I spoke about Mi'kmaq history with schoolchildren, my role as traditional leader and healer, and about my people today, to help them understand our way of life and hopes for the future.

As we travelled together across England, I saw and I felt the long history and the spirits of the European peoples and their relationship to the lands. I walked the grassy hills and felt the spiritual energy at Stonehenge and at Avebury, in the old churches and villages, and in their cemeteries. And I thought about my own history, the Mi'kmaq people, how we were like them but different. They left strong proof, in physical things, of their long presence on the land, and I wondered about what marks my own people's history on our land.

* * *

Our Stonehenge is our wigwam and our canoe, our whole history, and our use of the land, our claim to be protectors of the land, our spiritual connections. All are our Stonehenge. Without those, we would be nothing at all. That's why it is important to me.

From the beginning, for me, building a canoe was a kind of spiritual project that became clearer as it went on. It was a journey that I was taking as part of my own understanding of what I was going through and needed to do. And, as the project got further along, it became a spiritual one for the builders, too, at least some of them. I know one for sure. It was more than just building a boat. All sorts of other things were tied into the canoe. And a very special kind of thing was happening, even to the crew building it. And it was neat to watch it happen. Maybe it was a little easier for me because I knew what was happening and why.

Our early plans were picking out a shed and preparing steamers for steaming the wood for our canoe. I had visited Golden Lake, Ontario, one summer where they still made birchbark canoes. And ours would be birchbark, of course, and 20 feet or over. Our biggest problem then was to get our wood so we could make timbers. Pine, if we were going to use that, or cedar for the planks. We could buy pine from our own hardware store. But we had to wait till summer to gather spruce wood roots – we could not use nails – and wait till July for the birchbark. I had some of the other details for the design, partly in my head and partly in some magazines I had found.

Birch bark ready for the construction.

Collecting spruce roots.
("Hundreds of feet of spruce root were used in the canoe.")

Canoe under construction.

The symbolic eagle is an important addition.

The *Spirit Wind* is ready.

Spanning time: "We own both the birchbark canoe and the plane."
(Photograph 1999)

In the summer, 1996, our first attempt to build a canoe ourselves failed when the logs we had specially chosen, cut, and tied to the shore somehow went adrift one night and were lost. It seemed we just couldn't get it together. It was a lot of work. We gathered birch bark and things like that, but we weren't quite sure how to go about building it. But I was with people who worked with wood all the time, so we didn't see it as any great task. It just might take a little longer and we'd make some mistakes. We knew we could do it. We didn't give up.

The next year, our band was given responsibility for managing training dollars to be used for community-based projects related to multi-tourism packaging. It was an opportunity to do a cultural project like the canoe. That fit what we wanted to do. We found Renni Martin, master canoe builder from the Mi'kmaq reserve at Restigouche, Quebec, and brought him to Conne River. He had all the skills, and he had already built canoes for the Museum of Civilization in Ottawa. We hired three individuals from the community – Billy Joe, Donny Benoit, and Rick Jeddore – to work on the canoe. They have the kind of close connection to the land that we needed. And it all worked out. They are now the master canoe builders in Conne River.

It took 14 weeks to train the men for building. Part of the training was to actually build the canoe, and the other part involved going out and bringing back bear fat, and going out and guiding hunters to get moose or caribou for skins to use on the trip. We planned to have a caribou skin sail, and we needed one to kneel or sit on, and to lie on if we had to be out overnight for long periods at St. Paul's Island. A caribou skin was also for presentation to the Grand Chief in Nova Scotia.

The bear fat, mixed with the resin – it's called *var* – from spruce trees, was to seal the canoe's seams. That involved a ceremony in itself. When the bear was brought back, the crew cooked its meat, and it was given out to the canoe builders, but I took none. So we needed a space for that, and for a fire outside to steam and bend the timber and spruce roots for lacing the bark to the frame. The canoe we built is more traditional than the one I saw at Glenbow Museum. That one had nails in it. Ours has none. Hundreds of feet of spruce root hold it together.

So many things took place over those 14 weeks, and sometimes it seemed a strange way to build a canoe, because it involved so much. But it all made it more meaningful for everyone. And, too, we had to find the right spot for entering the water to launch our craft. At one place I found, I felt the hair on the back of my neck stand up. I felt sparks go up my arm, and I realized it was a perfect place.

* * *

Voyages. *In the beginning of the canoe project, we planned to bring the canoe from Nova Scotia to Newfoundland. Our talk focused on how, in the past, our people had been coming from Cape Breton to Newfoundland. There wasn't much emphasis on making a trip back. Later, we began to realize that we had to think about how our Mi'kmaq people went both ways, not just one way. Newfoundland had always been a part of Mi'kmaq territory, so they had to travel both ways. So we decided then that we were going to go from Newfoundland back to Nova Scotia. And we*

*wouldn't bring the boat back. Making the trip
over was the important thing. We could complete
the whole circle – travel from Cape Breton to
Newfoundland – later.*

When we launched the Renni Martin canoe that fall, it was too
narrow. It was a fantastic model, but was it practical? It was
perhaps more along the lines you would put in a museum. We
really worked hard trying to keep it upright. Our first test in the
water was with one of the MPs from Ottawa, so we were frightened to death that we would dump this fellow in the bay.
Maybe we should have!

Trial run of canoe with guest Newfoundland MP Roger Simmons.

Later the next summer – that was 1998 – we took the
canoe to Flat Bay, in St. George's Bay, to see how it would fare
in the ocean. On the first trip out it was so unsteady that we
couldn't keep it upright; we capsized and found out it was too

narrow. But nobody got drowned or hurt. So we brought it back. I had a visit with Charlie Labrador, a canoe builder from Nova Scotia. He told me a story that when Mi'kmaq people wanted to store their canoes for the winter months, they wouldn't store them on land. They would sink them in the ocean, in the lakes. That way they would be nice and flexible, and they wouldn't freeze and dry. So I said, "Well, we'll do the same thing." We took ours up to the park, filled it with sandbags, and sunk it in the water.

Two weeks later somebody called me and said, "Your canoe is on the shore." I don't know how it came up, but it was sitting there on the beach when I got there, and in the cold water it had gotten wider. It had gone from a 35-inch beam to about 45 inches. It was perfect. And that's how we got to fix our canoe – by sinking it in the lake without knowing what we were doing, except to store it. It fixed itself! But we decided the canoe was too small, so over the winter we built another for eight paddlers.

So that was the canoe that we later took across to Nova Scotia, at least partways. We started out from Cape Ray, the traditional landing place when coming from Nova Scotia. Cheeseman Park, at Port aux Basques, is a beautiful place to land, with sandy beaches when you come into the river there. Years ago it must have been like a grocery store, with eels and shellfish, caribou and mountains. Coming from Nova Scotia, they'd first land at St. Paul's Island, then paddlers would be sent on ahead to Cape Ray, where they would light a fire on a mountaintop to guide the following crews across. So we'd go back the same way across the Cabot Strait.

It was about 14 hours from the time we left Cape Ray, Newfoundland, and we were in sight of St. Paul's Island, when a storm broke. We were helped by a motor vessel that followed us in reaching the island, but lost the canoe. Pat Hanks went back to pick up the Renni Martin canoe we left behind. He brought that canoe to Nova Scotia by ship, and then we paddled it back to St. Paul's Island, and finally back to Nova Scotia. Our goal was get to Chapel Island in the Bras d'Or lakes, where all the Mi'kmaq nation gathered on Mission Day, July 26. We had lost time, so when we landed in Nova Scotia, we overlanded the canoe from there to Seal Island Bridge, the one just before you go up to Kelly's Mountain. We put our canoe in the water there and went on to the Bras d'Or lakes, up to Chapel Island. And we got there the day before Mission Day. We're proud that an award-winning film was made of the voyage.*

There's much I could say about learning to understand how our ancestors voyaged back and forth, and the 33-foot birchbark canoe that we built and took out to St. Pierre-Miquelon. We paddled along the shoreline from Conne River to Pass Island, then south over 21 miles of water to Miquelon. We travelled only when the tide was going out.

It took three years to build our canoes and make the first trip to Cape Breton. Three seasons, all during our holidays, and we had to try to do this in the space of four weeks. For any community, building something like this is a challenge – it hadn't been done in living memory – but it pulls everyone together. It was slow to catch on. But I went to the school and invited the teachers to bring their class to view the canoe being built, and by the time it was finished, everyone was involved and there to greet the paddlers coming back from trial runs. We had two

* Catherine Martin's documentary *Spirit Wind* (2000).

physically disabled children in the community, and we took them both for rides in the canoe. We also took it into the gymnasium, where the children came together to view the canoe up close. If the canoe project was pretty much mine in the beginning, it became a community project, not the chief's.

Not everybody sees the same thing in the canoe as I do, but they're aware that it's a craft that was built by our people, and it's part of our visual history. It has links to our past. And our craftspeople appreciated the skills involved. It was amazing to watch them work and create art on the paddles. The pride in what they were doing showed in their faces. It showed in the people around them, like their friends and family. It showed in the kids that greeted them. It all came together in that way.

Visiting Mi'kmaq craftsman fashioning a canoe paddle.

* * *

The Pow-wow connects us to the past. *An important part of redeveloping our traditions are the inter-tribal Pow-wows at Conne River, the first in July 1996. It brought a lot of our people closer together.*

Poster advertising first Conne River Pow-wow in 1996.

Mi'sel Joe at Pow-wow 2000. The summer event involves integrative social, cultural and spiritual ceremonies and activities. It is open to young and old, aboriginal and non-aboriginal.

> *It helps us build on what we have, such as our*
> *ladies' dancing group. It's always at the Pow-wow.*
> *It has helped us jump pretty high in the last years.*

I was reluctant to have the Pow-wow at first, because I was unsure how our own people would react to it. But I finally said, "To hell with it. Let's do it and see what happens." It was amazing to see our children come out to dance in their regalia. And they drew in their parents. The first year, you'd see parents hanging outside the fence, and the next year they started to show up with their own regalia. And their grandparents, my father, my uncle.

Another project involves at least seven or eight young women learning to make traditional Mi'kmaq baskets. Maybe the basket-making project was overshadowed by the canoe project because they were running side by side, but it's an important part of our tradition.

Accommodation available at "wigwam hotel" during the 1998 Pow-wow.

* * *

Children must be part of our tradition. One reason why we built the canoe and undertook our journey to Nova Scotia was to capture history for our young people. They grow up with the knowledge that it was done, but only in stories. We wanted to bring that story to life and actually do it for our young people.

We try to involve our children in many ways. I can't convince everyone that what we did and are doing will help our communities, will bring people closer together. Teenagers are often harder to reach because they're at a pretty cocky stage. They don't like to be told what to do, where to go. But a lot of them were interested in the canoe, and some said they were willing to make the trip across the Gulf if we needed them, to be one of the team of paddlers. That was a good sign. But we only have room for a few, so we drew names. We didn't want to dampen people's spirits. If anyone wanted to go, then we had to find a way to make them feel like they were part of it.

Bringing traditions alive helps to supplement the school curriculum. I've gone into the school and helped with the drums and stuff like that. But there is always more to do. Every department in our band needs to be looking after traditional things in terms of their own job, that would be through our actions, our job creation, our social services. Everything we do has to touch our traditional ways of living in some way for our people. When people appreciate their own history, that's healthy. It helps them feel good when they better understand their history and what it teaches them. The more people appreciate and believe in the same things, have the same good feel-

Brenda Jeddore rehearsing choir at St. Anne's School, 1990s.

A scene from the school's Pow-wow. ("It's exciting that our school is teaching the children our culture. And sometimes it's the children that bring their parents to the community Pow-wow.")

ings about what's happening, the better they feel about themselves and their community.

And the school, with the choir, the drums, and the music, are very much part of rebuilding our credibility as a community. We are proud of the choir, the CD that was produced, the awards they win, and that they will be performing at the opening ceremonies of the 2010 Winter Olympics in British Columbia. It took time. Living in an aboriginal community,

---

Misel Joe's Liner notes for CD of the The Sipu'ji'j Drummers and Se't A'newey Kina'matino'kuom Choir

MIAWPUKEK – Conne River

Pjilatsi (Welcome). The Mi'kmaq songs and chants contained herein represent a big part of what we are about, as Miawpukek Mi'kmaq. They represent our history, culture, traditions and spiritual beliefs. Moreover, these songs and chants ensure our continued survival and existence as Mi'kmaq. We are a part of a great nation, the Mikamaw Nation, comprising what is known today as Newfoundland, Nova Scotia, New Brunswick, Eastern Quebec, Prince Edward Island and parts of Maine. Collectively, this area is referred to as Mi'kma'kik which means land for the Mi'kmaq. In Ktaqamkuk (Newfoundland), our relative isolation from the rest of the Mi'kmaq Nation leaves us feeling lonely and separated at times. This, coupled with outside influences that served to erode our culture and traditions, makes our struggle for survival a great challenge. In recent years a resurgence of pride and dignity in our history and traditions has resulted in the revival of our language and cultural practices. The songs and chants as performed by the Sipujij Drummers and the Set A'newey Kina'matino'Kuom Choir (St. Anne's School) are a direct result of this resurgence. Today, just as in the past, our resolve to survive as Mi'kmaq is as strong as ever.

This compact disc represents a major accomplishment in preserving and promoting our language, customs and traditions. As Saqamaw of the Miawpukek Mi'kmaq, I would like to thank the Mi'kmaq performers and all those who helped make this product a success. As well, a special thanks to our elders, the composers of the song and chants, and to the rest of our great nation for helping us restore these traditions at Miawpukek.

I am confident that all, Mi'kmaq and non Mi'kmaq, will enjoy this compact disc and in the process gain greater appreciation of who we are as Miawpukek Mi'kmaq.

We'lalin' Saqamaw Mi'sel Joe (Traditional Chief)

---

people are not always happy to see their children go outside. You don't know what might happen to them. But the benefits for the children help to meet that and help us to lay a good, solid road to what we want to do.

* * *

Many of our traditions are coming alive again. Once you know one traditional person, you are pointing in the direction of a hundred people that can help you in your quest for more knowledge about what you're doing.

In this way, one is always learning. And one finds new people come on stream, on board looking for information. It's sort of a magical thing.

Revitalizing traditions. Mi'sel Joe talking with students at St. Anne's School about Mi'kmaq history and culture.

Developing self-government had many strands. A photograph of Judge Robert Fowler with members of the community on the occasion of holding court at Conne River (1980s). The judge's robe, with Mi'kmaq symbols, was made for the occasion.

4

Community Services

Spiritual and community journeys. My spiritual journey has only been partly through traditional ways. It is also with people, their values, inside and outside the community. I used to think that my spiritual experiences were over here and my community experience over there. But I've come to realize that it was all the same. The two mix together. I don't think you can separate a spiritual journey from a community journey or community work. And my community journey is along with many people on the same road. All that has happened in the Conne River community is a team effort, due to the work of many people, good people.

WE HAVE COME a long way from when my grandmother died of tuberculosis, for which she received very little care except from the family around her, and the days when the *Christmas Seal* came to Conne River as I mentioned earlier. Of course, we are still not a healthy community in the sense, for instance, that we still don't know why there is a high level of diabetes. We still don't know why all these things are happening to us, and I don't want to sugar-coat anything. We have problems as in other communities. But while we work at economic sustainability, we have been developing a variety of community services necessary to support a healthy and working community.

* * *

The Clinic is the hub of much of our community services. It is a key part of the Conne River Health and Social Services. We have a nurse practitioner, a full-time dental therapist and other staff, and a physician visits twice a week. But we also have the home care workers, and a daycare operating from the Clinic. The children's services – preschool daycare – and services for seniors are primarily run by the Clinic.

The Clinic is always busy. Our people have come from living off the land right up to the early '60s, and all of a sudden we're into store-bought foods, can foods, and stuff like that. And we're seeing the effects of that. We have, as I said, a problem with diabetes. It's not quite as bad as the national average, perhaps because we still eat a lot of traditional food, a lot of fish, wild meats, and berries. But it's still coming more and more to the younger Mi'kmaq. They're more into fast foods. So I fear we'll eventually catch up to the rest of the nation.

The Clinic and our Wellness Centre both deal with diabetes, trying to help people maintain a healthy diet and exercise. The Wellness Centre was opened primarily to take care of elders. It started out as an illness centre, but over time most people go in to talk about diets, weight, and stuff like that. It's managed from the Clinic, but in a separate building. A nurse practitioner helps there, along with a public health nurse and a nursing assistant. They do a good job in terms of promoting prevention, with people going for tests on a regular basis. As soon as someone gets sick, they've got to be tested for diabetes.

Our staff is generally from the community. (We're proud that Ada Benoit Roberts was the first Mi'kmaq person to graduate as a nurse practitioner.) Over the years, we wrote into our policies that anyone coming into the community from outside to work does so on a year-by-year contract.

I'm coming now to modern-day healers or doctors. I seriously believe that if I went to hospital and if I wasn't treated according to some of my beliefs, I would suffer. If I showed up at the hospital with my feather, my sweetgrass, the things that I believe in, if I wasn't allowed to keep these things with me as part of my own healing, I believe that a doctor could do serious harm to me. Modern-day medicines are fine medicines, but there's something else that goes along with that. Treatment is far more than handing out pills. It's the way the doctor hands you those pills, it's how he receives you in his clinic, how he is able to relate to some of the things you are talking about.

An important part of the work surrounding the Clinic is promoting health awareness in the school. They serve a healthy snack meal in either the morning or afternoon, and they don't allow soft drinks, like Pepsi, in the school. Only juice or water. The students go home for lunch, so there's nothing you can do to control that end, except try to ensure that both parents have access to jobs and access to healthy food. There's enough literature floating in the community to let them know what a

The Band Council Building, centre of initiatives and programs.

healthy diet should be, and a dietitian visits the community on a monthly basis to meet anyone who wants to talk to her.

The local store is important indirectly for health. It's run by John Jeddore. He's 86 years old now, and comes from a time when all you needed were the basics to get by on; he's maintained that in the store to some degree. But his grandsons are taking on the store, so that's likely to change with regards to what the community needs. The wife of one of the grandsons is from the United States, and it seems she's going to bring in some of the new healthy foods, which is great for the community. I'm now in my early 60s and go in for a regular checkup. I work a lot and I try to eat good food. I eat a lot of fish. I don't eat a lot of red meat anymore. My diet is fish, fish, fish.

* * *

> **Child and youth services.** *In the same building as the Clinic we have Miawpukek Child and Family Services; it provides programs to both children and elders. Inside the building we have a fully functioning playroom for children, part of our daycare program. When we were building the Clinic, we had the children paint pictures on the basement walls.*

It's not uncommon for adults to walk in and take part in the services that we provide, to play with the children. I like to get involved with some of their discussions and play. It's very humbling and very rewarding at the same time.

And since 2004 we have a Youth Centre – the Cecil Benoit Youth Centre – that's also operated by the Clinic. It's named after a Conne River elder, who died about 20 years ago, because he was a very good family person and had a big family. He always had a lot of kids around and took care of them.

The Centre is in two separate buildings. One building is on the other side of the school and operated by staff. It closes at ten o'clock at night. Different staff run it for youth all day long, even during school hours, for some kids have different classes. So if they're not in school they can go there. It's a safe place for them; not everybody wants to be out on the parking lot.

It's not a place for introducing traditional Mi'kmaq culture. They haven't done that yet. At this stage, it is primarily just a place for young people to hang out at night, if they need to be out. They have pool tables and games in there. We don't have a hockey rink, but we're hoping to build one. Right now, floor hockey is played in the gym, and we skate on the bay ice during the winter months. A lot of our kids also go to St. Alban's or down to Harbour Breton to play in competitions.

* * *

Our elders are as important to us as our children. We know through our own history how we should be looking after elders and seniors. We know that if you take them from the community into some clinic or hospital away from the family, that it may kill him or her. So, as a community, as leaders and healers in the community, we need to take control of that and ensure that we do everything we can within the community system itself to provide every service possible to ensure that people stay. We try to cover every health concern.

For us, anybody over 60 is considered a senior. I've had this conversation often with some of our older people, and tell them, "You're not elders. You're senior citizens." An elder is only someone that's selected by the community and given that role. But most of them don't want to acknowledge that. Everybody wants to be an elder. That's fine, too.

Some years ago we developed a program for elders and seniors who live alone. For someone to go in to visit them, talk with them, do basic cleaning and cook good meals. We identified that a number of them living alone had special dietary requirements as a result of diabetes and hypertension, so we provided cooked meals suited to their diet from the Clinic's

A calendar recognizing the knowledge and experience of elders.

Nutrition Centre. We didn't want to just feed them bologna, although *I* think that is good food!

But the Centre has changed somewhat. It still serves community visitors but, nowadays, it spends much time preparing healthy snacks for school. And they also cater for different functions throughout the year to Band members. It is a service managed by the Clinic in a separate building with staff year-round – nutrition workers who have been trained and certified to deal with foods and to cook. What happened is that many elders were saying, "We don't like the food. It don't taste right." They were healthy meals, but the elders were used to a lot of salt, and everything. And we found out through our own surveys that a lot of those meals were finding their way out to the dogs and cats. And the other thing we found out was they liked the service primarily for company. When somebody brought the meal he or she would sit down and have a chat, because part of the job was to see how you're doing. So the meals were more important for company rather than the meal itself.

So the program was revised; in other ways we all take up the slack in getting around and visiting people to help reduce this loneliness feeling. That is in addition to the home care program offered through the Wellness Centre, 24 hours a day in some cases. Some of the home care workers are from Conne River, and some are people we hire from around the area. It all depends on who has the training for it. And that works really well. As for visiting, we all agreed that we would try to maintain the social connections. This is better now than before, because we're more conscious of their importance.

It's so easy to be lonely, so easy to get sick from loneliness, so we maintain contact. We know when birthdays roll around or when it is a special day; we make sure that a postcard or a birthday card goes out to maintain that contact. During the Christmas season, the Band Council staff might take Christmas presents around. There will be people from the school who do the same thing. And it doesn't only apply to elders, but also to anyone who lives alone. It could be a 16-year-old to a 95-year-old. And we know if a person has a history of alcoholism and locks himself in his house, so someone will check every day to make sure everything is as it should be.

If you are living alone, there's a helmet of loneliness that you must go through. Helping with this is a form of healing in itself.

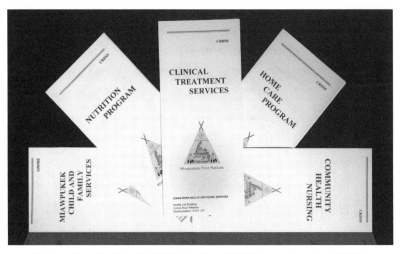

Information leaflets highlighting Band Clinic's services (c. 1998).

As chief, not only do I visit, but I also manage a small repair project, so that we can have some funds all year long if someone needs a refrigerator or a stove, or if something happens that they need over the winter months when all the regular projects are shut down. We still manage that through my office. We do minor repairs, like for broken windows, roof leaks, or maybe their steps are not in good shape, etc. We do all those things through a small budget. This year we're a little bit better off. We managed to get some money from our shrimp fishing program to put into an elders project.

The Clinic's mission statement is to address the health, social, and survival needs of the residents of the reserve in a manner "that teaches self-reliance, strengthens families and promotes community values of mutual support, sharing, and togetherness."

* * *

When an elder walks through the door he has probably swallowed a lot of pride. *Like all types of institutions that start to get bigger and broader, one matter with which we have concern is to bring along the staff at the same speed, to make them appreciate that when an elder walks through the door, he has probably swallowed a lot of pride to do so. And when he gets in the door, he's got to feel comfortable. He knows full well that when he gets to see the doctor (or someone else in authority), he is meeting someone that should be given a lot of respect, but he also has to feel comfortable in that building.*

Treatment, as I said, is far more than handing out pills. It's the way the doctor *hands* you those pills, it's how he receives you in his waiting room, it's how he receives you in his clinic, it's how he is able to talk to make you feel comfortable, how he is able to relate to some of the things you are talking about. It may not be that I've got a sore finger, but that I've got something in here – my spiritual part – that's bothering me as well. He's got to be able to deal with the finger and with my spiritual part in a nice and friendly way.

And when I walk out through the door, I need to feel healthier, to have things under control. And it is important to be able to walk out into a community that supports you. That spiritual help comes from a number of sources, from the community, from the leaders of the community, from different lay people. I hope we are doing that.

* * *

We built what we called a "Spiritual Building." We built it hoping that people will use the building to unload and have a healthier family, a healthier lifestyle; indeed, to become a healthier worker who's going to be able to make a long-lasting contribution to the overall health of all of us. It allows people to get together free from politics, free from the everyday hang-ups that we may have. I may not like the colour of your coat or I may not like the way you look, but once we walk into this little building, then you hang what you call your monkey on the nail outside. There's no place for it inside.

Very simply, the building is small enough that people can sit across from each other and talk to each other without having to

The "Spiritual Building" (photograph 1998).

raise voices. The central fireplace is the focal point of the building itself. The lighting is such that it's not directly on your face, but on your back. It's comfortable. We have encouraged everyone to come into the building, to use the building at storytelling time, to have children come into the building to sit with elders and listen to their stories.

* * *

We no longer have our own police. We dismantled that a few years ago, though as I mentioned earlier, we have sentencing circles. Having our own police was one service that didn't work out as well as we wanted it to, and the community thought that we should go back to the RCMP. So we now have an RCMP station in Conne River. It's easy to work with them, and, fortunately, there's not a lot of crime in Conne River. We still don't lock our doors at night.

Probably the main reason why our own police didn't work out – and it has been the same elsewhere, as I gather from police officers in other bands – is that it's really difficult to police your own people. It causes more social problems than it creates goodwill. Say, if you have to arrest your brother for drinking and driving, you're attacking the whole family. And then it creates social problems. We had one member of our community force who, from day one, was fighting his family all the time. His mom got involved, and his dad and brothers. And it can get ugly after a while. The poor officer was trying to do his job and trying to be impartial – it was pretty difficult.

* * *

Employment is one of the most important aspects of a person's dignity. *The Band Council works very hard at doing everything it can to make sure that everyone in the community can have a job. We provide jobs. We don't ask anyone, "Do you want to go to work?" We have a lady that calls on a regular basis to say, "Well, I found another job for you." It may be working at the warehouse, with the garbage collection system, perhaps with the security system, or with something else within the band suitable for the individual. But they are given a choice.*

I believe one reason for our community's development is our efforts to employ everybody in a family. Nothing is worse than having nothing to do and watching everybody else go to work and make a decent living, and buy things that they want or need. So we set out to employ every person who wants to work. At the same time, we're cautious about a young person going into the job creation that we set up and not go to high school. So we start them at a lower wage, primarily to encourage them to go back to school and to go to university. We really have some good programs for university and technical training. We say to people, "You find a university that'll take you. If it's something you can't find in Newfoundland, we don't care what part of the world it's in, we'll try to get you there if it's in our power." And it's the same for technical training.

The employment programs are done through our Program Services at the high school and our Human Resources. Some people work on different projects during the year. These projects are set so that the right people work at them, people who are experienced or who are good at that particular kind of work. We also include mentally challenged people, fit them into the project, let them do the work that needs to get done. Most projects run anywhere from 14 to 17 weeks at different times of the year. Everybody has the opportunity to have a house. It's sharing in the wealth – I guess you want to call it that – with everybody else."

* * *

Developing life skills is important for our community. I mentioned earlier that we took over

the school from the Church. We knew what had
to be done was better than existed.

We changed the school curriculum a bit; we began to teach the
Mi'kmaq language and about our culture. I knew that about
220 band-run schools throughout Canada, and the reserve
schools in Nova Scotia, taught their own history and everyone
co-operates to make it successful. We knew the quality of our
education would be better, equal to what the province offers,
and we expected our graduates could qualify for university.

But not everybody will come out with a grade 12, so, outside the school itself, we had programs in life skills that would
be very helpful to them, like carpentry and heavy equipment
operation. For that we used shadow management right in the
community. Unskilled young people worked with band members already trained in different occupations. And even older
people were retrained. It gradually evolved to include instruc-
tion in how to fill out applications for work and how to be good
members of the community. And we encouraged people to train
for more technical pursuits, for instance, helicopter pilot
training, even if they had to be sent away to school for the
skills. Several adults enrolled in Adult Education courses at our
school during the evening. When they finished their Level III,
they went on to post-secondary institutions for trade, business
and other courses; they're now working in the Band Clinic,
Wellness Centre, Daycare, Youth Centre, and band businesses.
We were educating the community. And today we have computers in the school and a payroll deduction program to get
computers into our homes for kids. And now, in 2009, almost
everyone uses them.

* * *

Job creation means we have to be entrepreneurs in developing projects. This goes for the Band Council and individuals.

The Council always has a number of projects. Mine are more along the lines of cultural development, but others are on economic development, though the distinction is not always sharp. We have an incredible team of people helping to build our economy.

Our recent brochure calls on businesses and communities to partner with us in tourism/recreation, aquaculture, construction, commercial fisheries, offshore oil/supply, and mineral exploration. Also listed are some examples of businesses owned and operated by the Band that show how we, the Miawpukek First Nation, link traditional knowledge with economic opportunity: Christmas tree farming, Conne River Outfitters, Glenn John Crafts Development Centre, Jipujij'kuei Kuespem Nature Park, Netukulimk Fisheries Ltd, silviculture, and ecotourism.*

To mention developing tourism – it covers cultural and economic development. I have in mind building this humongous dream catcher as a tourist attraction! Seriously, we've done some practical projects. We have had one cruise ship visit the reserve, and we hope to have more. That visit happened because of our connection with St. Pierre-Miquelon. We put on

* *Miawpukek First nation. Renewing Our Destiny. Come Explore the Miawpukek First Nation. Partner with Us As We Share Our Community With You, 2007.*

a really good show for them – like a mini Pow-wow – to let them know that this is not just another Newfoundland community. It is an aboriginal community. And from that they want to come back. We have never had a wharf, but hope to have one soon. Our community also looks for economic benefits through selling our crafts and stuff like that.

Entertaining the captain of a cruise ship (2007).

We just took over ownership of the Interpretation Centre that was recently built on the corner where the road to St. Alban's turns off the Harbour Breton highway. I don't know that it will be a museum – something I've wanted for some time. It'll certainly have more exhibits from our community, but it represents the whole region.

We are pleased that we now have offices in the province of the organization called Ulnooweg Development Group. It started as a Nova Scotia organization made up of chiefs from Atlantic Canada, excluding Newfoundland. Eight or nine years ago, I went and had a meeting with Chief Jerry Paul, who was the chair of that organization, and asked him to consider allowing that group to come to Newfoundland. After a lot of discussion, he agreed that it would be good to set up in Newfoundland. And we now have an office in St. John's, another in Goose Bay, and they're doing incredible business. We were pleased to have the annual awards show in St. John's in 2007 to recognize the work that Ulnooweg is doing in the aboriginal communities, highlighting some of the young people who are able to move forward under that fund. It makes loans, not grants. And it's working quite well.

* * *

The Band Council's projects must have the support of band members. The bottom line is that the grassroots people lead the charge, because it's their process. The chief and band council work for the community.

Way back in the 1970s, we had consultation meetings with the community to put together a road map to follow in terms of self-government. That allows the community to play a major role. Meetings continue and encourage band members to play lead roles in that process. It brings traditionalists together with the non-traditionalists and the fence-sitters. And we treat every idea or question put forward as good. And that idea or question is explored and, however long it takes, when band members are happy with the process, it's ready to happen. Today we still work very hard to be sure we communicate with our band members and with the outside. We fine-tune our communication skills, because that gives us strength.

Revitalizing traditions. Mi'sel Joe at work on a canoe paddle (1996).

Opening of the new Parks Canada Interpretation Centre on the Great Northern Peninsula, near Gros Morne. Shown are Mi'sel Joe, Sandra Kelly, and Gerry Byrne. (1997 photograph)

5

Journeys and the Future

My journey has really been many journeys. They have been personal and with the community. A journey to learn about myself as a Mi'kmaq person in Newfoundland and Canada. A journey to recognize that all of us are taught by everyone around us. A journey to bring Conne River to the chiefs of Canada. Canoe journeys to show how we are connected with the Mi'kmaq of Nova Scotia, and to show that St. Pierre and Miquelon are part of our historical network. Our travel has helped us break out of isolation. We know the only way to do that is to get out and meet people, the good, bad, and the ugly. And, in some ways, my journey has been the same kind as that of Sylvester Joe, when he was guiding William Cormack in his famous walk across Newfoundland in 1822 – showing people who we are and what we know.

AS TIMES CHANGE, so do our personal journeys. I hope to continue, like others in our community, to be an ambassador to let people know that we don't have to give up our language and culture, as happened in the past. We live in modern society; we are both like everybody else and different.

The role of community ambassador offers many opportunities.
Mi'sel Joe greets Pope John Paul II in St. John's in 1984.

We have been showing and sharing our Mi'kmaq culture in many ways and places, not just in Conne River. In May 1997, our exhibition at the Arts Resources Centre in St. John's helped us to break out of our isolation. Its theme was "Let's all come together and be friends." It meant let's all respect each other and each other's differences. Let's build on what we have, for we share this land and its resources. Let's support each other. The exhibition helped us show people that we are both very much in the twenty-first century and connected to our past, and that both must be focal points in our education.

Back in the early 1980s, I heard Chief Dan George for the first time. Part of his centennial message was: "We talk about what we used to have, we talk about the forest, we talk about the fish and the land, the Great Spirit. And we talk about the alcohol that came with the early Europeans. And we talk about being cheated." But then he finished, saying, "It's important to understand that our survival depends on the tools that were brought, the education that was offered," and "before we all go to this place called the Spirit World, we will see our young people change."

In my personal journey I hope I can influence our children about our roots and traditions. I am writing about the 1822 journey of Sylvester Joe with Cormack, and I am also writing more children's stories to follow my little book, *Muinji'j Becomes a Man*, which was published in 2003. It, too, is about a journey, one in which Muinji'j has to face the challenges and mysteries of a city he has never seen and return to help his grandfather and his village that relies on him.

The journeys of us all at Conne River have many hurdles ahead, as do all rural communities in Newfoundland. Our land claim will continue, although we lost that in the Supreme Court of Newfoundland and the Supreme Court of Canada refused to hear our appeal. So we'll have to find another route to go back. It means we don't have enough information, and we'll have to go back again to our proposals and research. We're hoping to find more information somewhere related to Mi'kmaq people in early Newfoundland.

We all have high points in our journeys. I wished the whole community could have been with me when I received an honorary doctorate from Memorial University in 2004. To me it was the sense of accomplishment, not so much for me, but for all our people. Who in Conne River would have bet that 50 years later our journey would be watched by the type of learned people who had so much power over us when I was growing up?

* * *

You found two statements I had made in the past. In 1986, I was able to say, "People have realized it's great to be a Newfoundland Micmac. People are openly saying, 'Look, I'm a Micmac person.' I remember back a few years ago when the people were a little bit shy of being called Micmac. It came from the dirty things other people were saying about Micmacs."* And in 1997, I wrote, "The outlook for the Miawpuket Mi'kmaq is promising. We look to a future of prosperity and co-operation with federal and provincial governments and non-aboriginals."**

In the last 20 years and more, we have come a long way. The future remains promising as we continue to co-operate with governments, constitutions, companies, and individuals. And I will be travelling with the community on that path.

* T.M.T.C. News (Toqamkuka Mi'kamaw Tribal Council News) Issue #1, July 16, 1986.

** Booklet from Band Council, *Miawpukek Mi'kmaq*, 1997.

Entrepreneurship. SCB Fisheries (c. 2000) at a time of partnership with Conne River Band.

Connections. Reconnecting with the French island of Miquelon in 2004. A delegation from Conne River; part of the festivities associated with a canoe journey from Conne River to Miquelon.

Acknowledgements

Special thanks to Colletta Joe for her steadfast support, Alma Benoit for faithful service over many years, and Linda MacDonald for sharing her experience as a band council member. Thanks also to Roberta Buchanan, Georgina Queller, Violette Ruelokke, Don Steele, and Geraldine Rubia, all members of the Newfoundland Writers' Guild, for helpful comments on early sections of this account. Roberta Buchanan suggested a comparison between Chief Joe's story and that of Northern Cree Chief Billy Diamond (see Further Reading). And sincere thanks to Garry Cranford, Jerry Cranford, and Margo Cranford of Flanker Press for their skills and enthusiasm, and for their strong commitment to building the heritage of Newfoundland and Labrador for future generations.

Bibliography

1. Sources cited in Chief Joe's story

Anger, Dorothy. "Putting it Back Together: Micmac Political Identity in Newfoundland." Masters thesis, Memorial University, 1983.

DeBlois, Albert D., and Alphonse Metallic. *Micmac Lexicon*. Ottawa: National Museums of Canada, 1984.

Jackson, Doug. *On the Country: The Micmac of Newfoundland*. St. John's: Harry Cuff Publications, 1993.

Joe, Mi'sel. *Muinji'j Becomes a Man*. St. John's: Breakwater Books, 2003.

Joe, Mi'sel. *"The Sipu'ji'j Drummers and Se't A'newey Kina'matino'kuom Choir*. Liner notes for the CD.

Martin, Catherine. *Spirit Wind*. 2000. A film documentary of the 1999 Conne River Mi'kmaq canoe journey across the

Gulf of St. Lawrence, from Cape Ray, Newfoundland, to Cape Breton Island.

Miawpukek Band Council. *Miawpukek Mi'kmaq.* Booklet, 1997.

Miawpukek Band Council. *Miawpukek First Nation/ Renewing Our Destiny/ Come Explore the Miawpukek First Nation/ Partner With Us As We Share Our Community With You.* Brochure, 2007.

Millais, J. G. *Newfoundland and Its Untrodden Ways.* London: Longmans Greene, 1907.

Prins, Harald E. L. *The Mi'kmaq: Resistance, Accommodation, and Cultural Survival.* New York: Harcourt Brace, 1996.

Whitehead, Ruth Holmes. *The Old Man Told Us: Excerpts from Micmac History 1600–1950.* Halifax: Nimbus Publishing, 1991.

T. M. T. C. News (Toqamkuka Mi'kama Tribal Council News), no. 1 (July 16, 1986).

2. Further Reading

Four brief expert summaries of literature on the Mi'kmaq people, with particular emphasis upon those in Newfoundland, are provided in Newfoundland and Labrador's Provincial Heritage website: (heritage.nf.ca/aboriginal/mikmaq_history.html). They treat, respectively, their history, traditional culture, the impact of non-aboriginal activities on them, and Mi'kmaq organizations and land claims. A select bibliography is included.

Additional relevant unpublished literature, including theses, dissertations, papers presented at conferences, and Newfoundland Mi'kmaq band newsletters and brochures, are archived at the Memorial University library in St. John's.

Mi'kmaq Diversity: Mi'kmaq bands are located in four provinces (Newfoundland, Nova Scotia, Prince Edward Island, and Quebec) and in the State of Maine. Their respective environments, histories, surrounding societies, and cultures differ despite a shared ethnic identity as members of one nation and similar experiences as aboriginal people in a White world. Harald E. L. Prins, in his *The Mi'kmaq: Resistance, Accommodation, and Cultural Survival* (New York: Harcourt Brace, 1996), offers a broad view of the Mi'kmaq nation and its changing culture since European contact. Literature cited leads to sources on many topics. Final suggestions follow.

A leader's testimony: As an oral history, Mi'sel Joe's story is one of many and varied personal accounts about the aboriginal encounter with and adaptation to white European colonization. They tell of aboriginal resistance, struggles to hold onto their traditional ways and values as European settlers and governments, driven by quite different visions, invade, plunder, settle, and transform their lands, sweep its original aboriginal occupants aside, and treat the survivors as if invisible or without the right to determine their own future.

Roy MacGregor's story, *Chief: The Fearless Vision of Billy Diamond* (New York: Viking Press, 1989), is an instructive comparison here. It speaks of Diamond's leadership among the James Bay Cree in Quebec from the 1960s through the mid-1980s. It was a turbulent period of struggle. It centres on the years during which Hydro Quebec and the Quebec Government undertook to transform the landscape they depended upon for their subsistence and living by a program of dam construction and flooding without first consulting the people dependent on the land affected. His story illustrates the continuing difficulties that First Nations people face in their relationships with governments and the dominant society around them, and the lengths to which Indian leaders and communities must go to gain control over their own futures.

Diamond's people organized themselves and resisted this development until they achieved an agreement with the developers and government that enables them to profit from it in ways that help sustain their independence on their terms. By contrast, politically unrecognized and unorganized, the interests of Newfoundland's Mi'kmaq did not figure in the Bay d'Espoir hydro development of the 1960s that flooded and reduced much of their traditional hunting and trapping lands and forests (see Jackson 1993: 168–169).

The stories of Billy Diamond and Mi'sel Joe demonstrate that aboriginal leaders can "turn things around," to their people's advantage in relationships with governments and surrounding communities and industries. Mi'sel Joe is one among contemporary Mi'kmaq leaders and their bands now working to sustain and build respect for their culture and heritage both within and without their communities. Albeit not without critics (see Oliver Moore, "Open for Business," *Globe and Mail*, December 12, 2008, p. B7). In addition to what Chief Joe tells us here, Canada's aboriginal people face continuing tensions between two contesting visions: autonomy vs. integration/assimilation. These tensions involve debate over such important issues as First Nation autonomy, treaty rights, aboriginal status rights, governance and representation, property rights, and education. These many concerns are discussed in *First Nations: Second Thoughts*, second edition (Montreal: McGill-Queen's Press, 1998) by political scientist Tom Flanagan.

An example of such tensions is met in recent media reports that the federal government is "secretly planning an overhaul of the rules governing Canada's reserves." (See Bill Curry, "Secret Documents Reveal Sweeping New Rules for Natives," *Globe and Mail*, March 3, 2009, p. A4).

Spiritual Values, Beliefs and Practices: Mi'sel Joe's own understanding of his people's traditional spiritual values, beliefs, and practices is patently fragmentary and changing. The same is true for the larger Mi'kmaq nation. After all, they live in many communities over five provinces and the state of Maine, and they exchange experiences and meet cultural ways of aboriginal peoples beyond their traditional boundaries. Likewise, Mi'kmaq culture in existing literature is diverse and changing. Traditions stand still for no one, although we often think and speak of them in that way. Yet even as they change, language and traditions more broadly bring and hold people together and create distinct social identities, and even movements.

Community Health and Aboriginal Canadians: A major reason for telling Chief Joe's story is his concern for action to restore and sustain his community's health. His specific health concerns are not unique among Canada's aboriginal people. In *Aboriginal Health in Canada* by James B. Waldram, D. Ann Herring, and T. Kue Young (Toronto: University of Toronto Press, 2008), readers will find a broad historical and cultural overview of health and illness issues, and traditional healing ways among Canada's aboriginal people. Mi'kmaq traditional medicine, from a Nova Scotian perspective, is described in Laurie Lacie's *Micmac Indian Medicine* (Antigonish: Formac, 1977).

Chief Joe's story illustrates his strong belief in the restoration or "cultural revitalization" of Mi'kmaq language, values, and spirituality to his people as fundamental to their health. (see R. R. Andersen, J. K. Crellin, and M. Joe, "Spirituality, Values and Boundaries in the Revitalization of a Mi'kmaq community," in Harvey, G. (ed). *Indigenous Religions: A Companion.* London: Cassell, 2000, pp. 243–254). This conviction is met widely among Canada's aboriginal people and in our literature. Two valuable examples are Wayne Warry's *Unfinished Dreams: Community Healing and the Reality of Self-Government* (Toronto: University of Toronto Press, 1998) and James B. Waldram's *The Way of the Pipe: Aboriginal Spirituality and Symbolic Healing in Canadian Prisons* (Peterborough: Broadview Press, 1997).

Alcohol (and drug) dependency and its many problems

are an especially prominent concern to aboriginal people across Canada. A highly insightful recent documentary account of their fight against it is given by Marie Wadden in *Where the Pavement Ends: Canada's Aboriginal Recovery Movement and the Urgent Need for Reconciliation* (Toronto: Douglas & McIntyre, 2008).

Two recent exemplars of the kind of intensive study needed to more fully grasp the structure and dynamic of Mi'kmaq traditions today are Anne-Christine Hornborg's *Mi'kmaq Landscapes: From Animism to Sacred Ecology* (Aldershot, England: Ashgate Publishing, 2008) and, with focus on Newfoundland's Mi'kmaq, Janice Esther Tulk's "Cultural Revitalization and Mi'kmaq Music-Making: Three Newfoundland Drum Groups." *Newfoundland and Labrador Studies* 22, no. 1 (2007): 259–285.

About Mi'sel Joe

Mi'sel Joe

CHIEF MI'SEL JOE is from a long line of Mi'kmaq saqamaws or chiefs. Raised in Conne River, he left school at the age of 14. At 16, he went to mainland Canada, where he was "educated" through a series of seasonal jobs, interlaced with hard times. He returned to Conne River in 1973 and quickly became involved in band politics, first as a councillor and, after the death of his uncle, Chief Billy Joe, in 1982, he was chosen traditional saqamaw. For many years he has also been elected administrative chief of the Conne River Reserve. His dual roles of spiritual leader and as administrator have given him a provincial and national voice that speaks to the needs of traditions and values in all societies. His awards and honours include an honorary doctor of laws degree from Memorial University and a Trudeau Mentor for 2009.

About the Editors

RAOUL R. ANDERSEN

JOHN K. CRELLIN

RAOUL R. ANDERSEN and **JOHN K. CRELLIN** are honorary research professors at Memorial University. Their backgrounds in anthropology, history, and medicine lie behind many collaborative activities. Ever since a Memorial University medical student undertook a project at Conne River in 1993, Andersen and Crellin have been involved with Mi'sel Joe in a variety of conferences and other educational activities.

Index

adult education, 143
alcoholism, 34, 37, 38, 42, 43, 67, 79, 100
alder leaves, 104
Ancelewit, 5, 43,
Anger, Dorothy, 157
armoured car, 24
Armstrong, Ontario, 28
Arts Resources Centre, 150
Assembly of First Nations, 51
ATVs, 84
Avebury, England, 109
Badger, 12
Band Council, 47, 64, 66, 69, 70, 95, 132, 137, 141, 144, 146, 152, 155, 158, 164
Band-run businesses, 143, 144
Band-run schools, 143
basket making, 90, 122
baskets, 90, 122
Bay d'Espoir, xv, xvi, 5, 8, 37, 160
Bay Nord, 99-102
Bay St. George Community College, 38, 39
bear, 26, 82, 87, 114, 115
bear fat, 114, 115
beaver, 11, 19, 20, 82, 83, 101

beaver root, 104
Benoit, Alma, 155
Benoit clan, 54, 114, 131, 133, 155
Benoit, Donny, 114
Benoit, Mike, 54
Bernard, Steve, 84
birch bark, 103, 110, 111, 113, 114, 118
Bishop's Falls, 37
blueberry leaves, 104
Bras d'Or lakes, 118
Buchanan, Roberta, 155
bundles, 84
Burke, Kitty, 85, 86
Cabot Strait, 117
Calgary, Alberta, 32, 34, 35, 107
Calgary Stampede, 33
canoe
    double-hulled, 108
    voyages, xix, 91, 108, 109, 115-119, 123, 149, 154, 157, 158
Cape Ray, 117, 118, 157, 158
catechism, 2, 6
Catholic Action Centre, 51
Cecil Benoit Youth Centre, 133

ceremonies
  Christmas wood burning, 96, 97
  give-away, 80
  healing, 76, 80, 81, 95, 104
  naming, 5, 60-62
  smudging, 78, 80
  sweetgrass, 78, 80, 106, 131
Chapel Island, 118
Cheeseman Park, 117
cherry bark, 88, 104
Child and Family Services, 133
children, xiv, 3, 5, 42, 51, 56, 76, 92, 98, 109, 118, 119, 122-126, 130, 133, 134, 140, 151
Christmas Seal, xii, 14, 15, 129
Christmastime, 34, 38, 40, 87, 96, 137, 144
Church, xii, xvi, 5, 51, 56, 79, 95, 106, 107, 142, 143
Churchill Falls, 37-41
clan, 16, 17, 60, 86, 87
Clinic and Wellness Centre, 66, 130-134, 136-139, 143
Clinic mission statement, 138
coffin makers, 94, 95
community ambassador, 149, 150
community police, 8, 140, 141
community projects, 108, 110, 114, 115, 119, 122, 137, 138, 142, 144, 146
community values, xi-xiii, xv, 75-127, 129, 138, 159-162, 164
compact disc, 107, 125, 157
computers, 65, 143
Confederation, xvi, 34
Cormack, William, 97, 98, 149, 151
Cornwallis, Edward, 7

Cross Brook, 100
cure, magical, 92, 99-102
curriculum, 123, 143
Curry, Bill, 161
daycare, 130, 133, 143
DeBlois, Albert D., 13, 157
dentist, 92
diabetes, 129-131, 134, 135
Diamond, William, 155, 160, 161
dietitian, 132
district chief, 47
doctor, 1, 1487, 89, 92, 95, 96, 100, 101, 131, 138
doctorate, honorary, 151, 164
Drew, George, 54, 98
Drew, Wilfred, 54
drumming, 95
drums, 95, 105-107, 123, 125, 157, 163
Dundas Street, 23
eagle, 60, 61, 77, 81, 83, 112
Eagle Island, 83
economic stability, xii, 130
Edison Hotel, 22
elders, 5, 60, 61, 78, 83, 92, 104, 125, 130, 133-140
employment, xiii, xiv, 32, 141, 142
Employment Insurance, 62
England, xiv, 109, 163
Eskasoni Reserve, 52, 69, 70, 77
fast, fasting, 53-55, 57-62, 66, 98, 99
Federal Native Peoples of Conne River Agreement, 49
fence-sitters, 146
Flanagan, Tom, 161
Flat Bay, 116
food, traditional, 11, 23, 26, 95, 98, 101, 130-132

Fort William, Ontario, 27
Fowler, Robert, 81, 128
French people, 21, 31, 32, 34, 35, 40, 154
Gander, 37, 56, 57
Gander River, 1
Gaultois, 14, 89, 90
George, Dan, 150, 151
George's Bank, 40
Gibbons, Rex, 83
gifts, 80, 86, 98, 99, 101, 102
Glenbow Museum, Calgary, 107, 115
Glenwood, 10-12, 18
Glooscap Cave, 102
Golden Lake, 110
Goose Bay, 146
Grand Banks, 40
Grand Chief, xiii, 47-49, 66-68, 70, 71, 114
Grand Falls, 38, 50, 65, 89
Great Spirit, 36, 64, 92, 150, 151
Greenway racetrack, 26
Gulf of St. Lawrence, 107, 157, 158
Halifax, Nova Scotia, 21, 22, 40, 158
Harbour Breton, 14, 89, 134, 145
Harvey, Graham, 162
Health and Social Services, 130
health awareness, 131
Health Sciences Centre, 101
Hermitage, 14
Herring, D. Ann, 162
High River, Alberta, 33, 34
Hinx, John, 84
homebrew, 7, 34, 87
home care, 130, 136
Hornborg, Anne-Christine, 163
hospital, cottage, 14, 89

house mortgage, 65
house, saltbox, 9
hunting, xv, xvi, 7, 10, 12, 19, 42, 82-84, 87, 114, 160
Hydro development, 38
Hydro Quebec, 160
hypertension, 134, 135
INCO, 36
Indian Act, xvi, 34, 48, 55
Interpretation Centre, 145
Jackson, Doug, 5, 157, 160
Jeddore, Brenda, 124
Jeddore, Gabriel, 100
Jeddore, John, 132
Jeddore, John Nicholas, 49
Jeddore, Martin, 10, 45, 48, 49
Jeddore, Melvin, 48
Jeddore, Noel, 5, 47, 52, 93
Jeddore, Paul Nicholas, 12
Jeddore, Rick, 54, 114
Jeddore, Sylvester, 14
Jeddore, Teresa, 100
job creation, 123, 142, 144-146
Joe, Amelia, 88, 89
Joe, Andrew, 12
Joe, Anne, 12
Joe, Aubrey, 54
Joe, Billy, 47, 49, 54, 93, 114, 164
Joe, Chesley, 54
Joe clan, x-xvii, 6, 12, 13, 16, 17, 33, 45, 47, 49, 51, 54, 55, 69, 88, 93, 97, 98, 108, 114, 121, 125, 127, 147, 149-151, 155, 157, 159-162, 164, 165
Joe, Colletta, 42-44, 62, 155
Joe, Harriet, 88
Joe, Lawrence, 12
Joe, Leona, 39, 42, 51
Joe, Molly, 89

Joe, Shannon, 42
Joe, Sului'an, 57
Joe, Sylvester, 97, 98, 149, 151
John clan, 10, 11, 50, 96, 101, 144
John, Marilyn, 50
John, Walter, 101
Kelly's Mountain, 118
Kenora, Ontario, 35, 36
Kent Street, 21
King's Ranch, 33
Ktaqamkuk, 125
Labrador, Charlie, 117
Lacie, Laurie, 162
Lake Nipigon, 28
Lake Superior, 27
land claim, xiv, 151, 159
Lever Brothers Mushroom Farm, 31
Lewis, Mary, 87
Lewis, Reuben, 88
life skills, 142, 143
Little Island, 57
little people, 97-99, 102
Little River, 85, 86
local store, 132
Lockporte, Nova Scotia, 40
loneliness, xv, 21, 26, 35, 72, 125, 136, 137
MacDonald, Angus, 21-23, 27
MacDonald, Linda, 66, 155
MacGregor, Roy, 160
Maine, 125, 159, 161
manitou, 88
Manpower, 23, 24, 26, 30, 36, 38
Maritime Provinces, x, xii, 5, 7, 13, 47, 48, 57, 60-62, 66, 68-70, 77, 78, 102, 107, 114-118, 123, 125, 143, 145, 146, 149, 159, 162

Marshall, Donald, 47, 71
Martin, Catherine, 118, 157, 158
Martin, Renni, 114, 116, 118
Matteau, 93
Maui, Hawaii, 108, 109
McNamara Marine, 40
medicine, cough, 88
medicine trail, 103
Members of Parliament, 116
Membertou Reserve, 69
Metallic, Alphonse, 157
Miawpukek First Nation, xi, 49, 73, 125, 144, 152, 158
Mick, Uncle, 93
midwife, xii, 13, 88, 89
Mi'kmaq prayer book, 92
Mi'kmaq values
    cultural identity, xv-xvii, 71, 72, 92, 97, 159
    dignity, xiii, 15, 25-27, 47-73, 75, 125, 141, 142
    language, xiv, 5, 7, 13, 49, 56, 59, 64, 71, 72, 76, 92, 93, 97, 125, 143, 149, 150, 162
Millais, J. G., 84, 158
Milltown, 4, 49
Milton, 30, 31
mindu, 58, 88, 99
Minister of Indian Affairs, 66, 67, 72
Miquelon, 90-94, 118, 144, 149, 154
Mission Day, 118
Mohawk territory, 69
molasses, 10, 88, 104
Montreal, 37, 161
Moore, Oliver, 161
moose liver, 7
Mount Sylvester, 97-99

mummering, 96

Museum of Civilization, Ottawa, 114

New Brunswick, xvii, 60-62, 125

Newfoundland government, xi, xii, xiv-xvi, 1, 6, 7, 18, 39, 48-53, 55, 56, 63-67, 75, 83, 85, 89, 152, 160

Newfoundland Tonto, the, 32-37

n'me, 13, 86, 87

n'me-tay, 87

non-traditionalists, xii, 146

Northern Construction Co., 38

North Sydney, Nova Scotia, 21, 68

Northwest River, 11

nurse, 14, 92, 131

nurse practitioner, 130, 131

nutrition, 66, 104, 135, 136

Nutrition Centre, 66, 135, 136

Olympics, 125

Ottawa, 66-69, 72, 114, 116, 157

Pacific sea, 108, 109

Pass Island, 118

Paul, Jerry, 146

Peckford, Brian, 55

Pepsi, 131

plants, medicinal, 102-105

Pope John Paul II, 150

Port aux Basques, 21, 37, 117

Portuguese people, 31

potatoes, 10, 105

Pow-wow, 120-122, 124, 144, 145

priest, xiv, 1, 5, 6, 11, 16, 18, 25, 56, 57, 91, 92, 95, 105, 106

Prince Edward Island, 125, 159

Prins, Harald E. L., 17, 158, 159

pulling together, 63-68

purification, 80, 99

Queller, Georgina, 155

railway

track, 27, 28

work, xv, 27-30, 41, 42

RCMP, 1, 7, 8, 36, 52, 140

Reeves, Mrs., 21

Regina, Saskatchewan, 36

registered aboriginal status, xvi

remote treatment centres, 80

repair project (home), 137, 138

respect, xii, 49, 52, 57, 73, 80, 82, 83, 86, 87, 99, 138, 150, 161

Restigouche Reserve, 69, 72, 114

revival, 102, 125

rifle, 12

Roberts, Ada Benoit, 131

root cellar, 10, 105

roots, 11, 104, 110, 111, 115

Ross, John, 55

Rubia, Geraldine, 155

Ruelokke, Violette, 155

St. Alban's, 3, 4, 85, 86, 91, 134, 145

St. Anne's Church, 93

St. Anne's Day, 16, 91, 105

St. Anne's School, 124, 125, 127

St. Anne's School choir, 124, 125

St. Croix, Stanley, xiv, 5

St. John's, 8, 50, 51, 65, 101, 105, 108, 146, 150, 157, 159

St. Paul's Island, 14, 117, 118

St. Pierre, 40, 118, 144, 149

Saqamaw, xi, 47, 93, 125, 164

school, 1-6, 12, 18, 32, 38, 41, 56, 66, 81, 91, 96, 105, 109, 118, 123-125, 127, 131, 133, 136, 137, 142, 143, 164

self-government, xii, xv, 146, 162

self-reliance, 138

senior citizens, 130, 134
senior services, 130, 134
sentencing circles, 81, 82, 140
Se't A'neway Kina'matino'kuom
    Choir, 125, 157
Seven Sorts, 104
shrimp fishing program, 138
Simmons, Roger, 116
Sipu'ji'j Drummers, 125, 157
Smallwood, Joey, 48
songs, 7, 13, 95, 96, 106, 125
spirit guide, 87
Spiritual Building, 139, 140
Spirit Wind, 113, 118, 157
spruce roots, 110, 111, 115
Steele, Don, 155
Stephenville, 38, 39
Stevens, Roddy, 52
Stonehenge, 109-115
storytelling, 97, 140
Sudbury, Ontario, 36, 37, 42
Supreme Court of Canada, 151
sweat lodge, 49, 57-59, 61, 70,
    76-81, 104
Talking Eagle, 60, 61
teenagers, 123
The Rooms, St. John's, 105
tomato sandwich, 24
Toronto, Ontario, 22, 24, 25, 27,
    28, 30, 35-38, 162, 163
tourism development, 114, 144
traditional chief, xi, xiii, 5, 47,
    52, 66, 125
traditionalists, xii, 146
traditional walk, 102
traditions, xi, xiv, xvii, 77, 90-92,
    102, 120, 123, 125-127, 147,
    151, 162-164
Trans-Canada Highway, 37
trapper incentive program, 83

trappers' association, 83
trapping, xv, xvi, 12, 19, 42, 68,
    82, 83, 85, 160
treatment, 5, 8, 79, 80, 131, 138
Trudeau Mentor, 164
tuberculosis, xii, 3, 14, 104, 129
Tulk, Esther, 163
turnips, 105
ulcers, 43, 100
Ulnooweg Development Group,
    145, 146
vandalism, 81
var, 114, 115
Vicks, 88
vision experience, 52, 53, 57-62
Wadden, Marie, 163
wakes, 86, 94-96
Waldram, James B., 162
Walk, the, 57, 68-73, 76
Warry, Wayne, 162
Welfare Department, 49, 62, 63
Wetzel, Jerry, 50, 51
White Caribou, 60-62
Whitehead, Ruth Homes, 7, 158
Wildlife Department, 83
Whycogomaugh, 72
Yonge Street, 22
Young, T. Kue, 162